D0778521

❖ ANCIENT WORLD LEADERS ❖

KING DAVID

◆◆◆

❖ ANCIENT WORLD LEADERS ❖

ALEXANDER THE GREAT
ATTILA THE HUN
CHARLEMAGNE
CLEOPATRA
CYRUS THE GREAT
DARIUS THE GREAT
GENGHIS KHAN
HAMMURABI
HANNIBAL
JULIUS CAESAR
KING DAVID
NEFERTITI
QUEEN OF SHEBA
RAMSES THE GREAT
SALADIN
XERXES

❖ ANCIENT WORLD LEADERS ❖

KING DAVID

LOUISE CHIPLEY SLAVICEK

Frontispiece: *King David. Limewood carving, circa 1470.*

For Debra J. Kraft

Chelsea House
An imprint of Infobase Publishing
132 West 31st Street
New York, NY 10001

Library of Congress Cataloging-in-Publication Data

Slavicek, Louise Chipley, 1956–
King David / Louise Chipley Slavicek.
p. cm. — (Ancient world leaders)
Includes bibliographical references.
ISBN 978-0-7910-9583-6 (hardcover)
1. David, King of Israel. I. Title. II. Series.
BS580.D3S485 2008
222'.4092—dc22
[B]

2008004868

Chelsea House books are available at special discounts when purchased in bulk quantities for businesses, associations, institutions, or sales promotions. Please call our Special Sales Department in New York at (212) 967-8800 or (800) 322-8755.

You can find Chelsea House on the World Wide Web at http://www.chelseahouse.com

Text design by Lina Farinella
Cover design by Jooyoung An

Printed in the United States of America

Bang NMSG 10 9 8 7 6 5 4 3 2 1

This book is printed on acid-free paper.

❖ CONTENTS ❖

Arthur M. Schlesinger, Jr.

On Leadership

Leadership, it may be said, is really what makes the world go round. Love no doubt smoothes the passage; but love is a private transaction between consenting adults. Leadership is a public transaction with history. The idea of leadership affirms the capacity of individuals to move, inspire, and mobilize masses of people so that they act together in pursuit of an end. Sometimes leadership serves good purposes, sometimes bad; but whether the end is benign or evil, great leaders are those men and women who leave their personal stamp on history.

Now, the very concept of leadership implies the proposition that individuals can make a difference. This proposition has never been universally accepted. From classical times to the present day, eminent thinkers have regarded individuals as no more than the agents and pawns of larger forces, whether the gods and goddesses of the ancient world or, in the modern era, race, class, nation, the dialectic, the will of the people, the spirit of the times, history itself. Against such forces, the individual dwindles into insignificance.

So contends the thesis of historical determinism. Tolstoy's great novel *War and Peace* offers a famous statement of the case. Why, Tolstoy asked, did millions of men in the Napoleonic Wars, denying their human feelings and their common sense, move back and forth across Europe slaughtering their fellows? "The war," Tolstoy answered, "was bound to happen simply because it was bound to happen." All prior history determined it. As for leaders, they, Tolstoy said, "are but the labels that serve to give a name to an end and, like labels, they have the least possible connection with the event." The greater the leader, "the more conspicuous the inevitability and the predestination of every act he commits." The leader, said Tolstoy, is "the slave of history."

Determinism takes many forms. Marxism is the determinism of class. Nazism the determinism of race. But the idea of men and women as the slaves of history runs athwart the deepest human instincts. Rigid determinism abolishes the idea of human freedom—the assumption of free choice that underlies every move we make, every word we speak, every thought we think. It abolishes the idea of human responsibility, since it is manifestly unfair to reward or punish people for actions that are by definition beyond their control. No one can live consistently by any deterministic creed. The Marxist states prove this themselves by their extreme susceptibility to the cult of leadership.

More than that, history refutes the idea that individuals make no difference. In December 1931 a British politician crossing Fifth Avenue in New York City between 76th and 77th Streets around 10:30 p.m. looked in the wrong direction and was knocked down by an automobile— a moment, he later recalled, of a man aghast, a world aglare: "I do not understand why I was not broken like an eggshell or squashed like a gooseberry." Fourteen months later an American politician, sitting in an open car in Miami, Florida, was fired on by an assassin; the man beside him was hit. Those who believe that individuals make no difference to history might well ponder whether the next two decades would have been the same had Mario Constasino's car killed Winston Churchill in 1931 and Giuseppe Zangara's bullet killed Franklin Roosevelt in 1933. Suppose, in addition, that Lenin had died of typhus in Siberia in 1895 and that Hitler had been killed on the western front in 1916. What would the 20th century have looked like now?

For better or for worse, individuals do make a difference. "The notion that a people can run itself and its affairs anonymously," wrote the philosopher William James, "is now well known to be the silliest of absurdities. Mankind does nothing save through initiatives on the part of inventors, great or small, and imitation by the rest of us—these are the sole factors in human progress. Individuals of genius show the way, and set the patterns, which common people then adopt and follow."

Leadership, James suggests, means leadership in thought as well as in action. In the long run, leaders in thought may well make the greater difference to the world. "The ideas of economists and political philosophers, both when they are right and when they are wrong," wrote John Maynard Keynes, "are more powerful than is commonly understood. Indeed the world is ruled by little else. Practical men, who believe themselves to be quite exempt from any intellectual influences, are usually the slaves of some defunct economist. . . . The power of vested interests is vastly exaggerated compared with the gradual encroachment of ideas."

But, as Woodrow Wilson once said, "Those only are leaders of men, in the general eye, who lead in action. . . . It is at their hands that new thought gets its translation into the crude language of deeds." Leaders in thought often invent in solitude and obscurity, leaving to later generations the tasks of imitation. Leaders in action—the leaders portrayed in this series—have to be effective in their own time.

And they cannot be effective by themselves. They must act in response to the rhythms of their age. Their genius must be adapted, in a phrase from William James, "to the receptivities of the moment." Leaders are useless without followers. "There goes the mob," said the French politician, hearing a clamor in the streets. "I am their leader. I must follow them." Great leaders turn the inchoate emotions of the mob to purposes of their own. They seize on the opportunities of their time, the hopes, fears, frustrations, crises, potentialities. They succeed when events have prepared the way for them, when the community is awaiting to be aroused, when they can provide the clarifying and organizing ideas. Leadership completes the circuit between the individual and the mass and thereby alters history.

It may alter history for better or for worse. Leaders have been responsible for the most extravagant follies and most monstrous crimes that have beset suffering humanity. They have also been vital in such gains as humanity has made in individual freedom, religious and racial tolerance, social justice, and respect for human rights.

There is no sure way to tell in advance who is going to lead for good and who for evil. But a glance at the gallery of men and women in Ancient World Leaders suggests some useful tests.

One test is this: Do leaders lead by force or by persuasion? By command or by consent? Through most of history leadership was exercised by the divine right of authority. The duty of followers was to defer and to obey. "Theirs not to reason why/ Theirs but to do and die." On occasion, as with the so-called enlightened despots of the 18th century in Europe, absolutist leadership was animated by humane purposes. More often, absolutism nourished the passion for domination, land, gold, and conquest and resulted in tyranny.

The great revolution of modern times has been the revolution of equality. "Perhaps no form of government," wrote the British historian James Bryce in his study of the United States, *The American Commonwealth*, "needs great leaders so much as democracy." The idea that all people should be equal in their legal condition has undermined the old structure of authority, hierarchy, and deference. The revolution of equality has had two contrary effects on the nature of leadership. For equality, as Alexis de Tocqueville pointed out in his great study *Democracy in America*, might mean equality in servitude as well as equality in freedom.

"I know of only two methods of establishing equality in the political world," Tocqueville wrote. "Rights must be given to every citizen, or none at all to anyone . . . save one, who is the master of all." There was no middle ground "between the sovereignty of all and the absolute power of one man." In his astonishing prediction of 20th-century totalitarian dictatorship, Tocqueville explained how the revolution of equality could lead to the *Führerprinzip* and more terrible absolutism than the world had ever known.

But when rights are given to every citizen and the sovereignty of all is established, the problem of leadership takes a new form, becomes more exacting than ever before. It is easy to issue commands and enforce them by the rope and the stake, the concentration camp and the *gulag*. It is much harder to use argument and achievement to overcome opposition and win consent. The Founding Fathers of the United States understood the difficulty. They believed that history had given them the opportunity to decide, as Alexander Hamilton wrote in the first Federalist Paper, whether men are indeed capable of basing government on "reflection and choice, or whether they are forever destined to depend . . . on accident and force."

Government by reflection and choice called for a new style of leadership and a new quality of followership. It required leaders to be responsive to popular concerns, and it required followers to be active and informed participants in the process. Democracy does not eliminate emotion from politics; sometimes it fosters demagoguery; but it is confident that, as the greatest of democratic leaders put it, you cannot fool all of the people all of the time. It measures leadership by results and retires those who overreach or falter or fail.

It is true that in the long run despots are measured by results too. But they can postpone the day of judgment, sometimes indefinitely, and in the meantime they can do infinite harm. It is also true that democracy is no guarantee of virtue and intelligence in government, for the voice of the people is not necessarily the voice of God. But democracy, by assuring the right of opposition, offers built-in resistance to the evils inherent in absolutism. As the theologian Reinhold Niebuhr summed it up, "Man's capacity for justice makes democracy possible, but man's inclination to justice makes democracy necessary."

A second test for leadership is the end for which power is sought. When leaders have as their goal the supremacy of a master race or the promotion of totalitarian revolution or the acquisition and exploitation of colonies or the protection of greed and privilege or the preservation of personal power, it is likely that their leadership will do little to advance the cause of humanity. When their goal is the abolition of slavery, the liberation of women, the enlargement of opportunity for the poor and powerless, the extension of equal rights to racial minorities, the defense of the freedoms of expression and opposition, it is likely that their leadership will increase the sum of human liberty and welfare.

Leaders have done great harm to the world. They have also conferred great benefits. You will find both sorts in this series. Even "good" leaders must be regarded with a certain wariness. Leaders are not demigods; they put on their trousers one leg after another just like ordinary mortals. No leader is infallible, and every leader needs to be reminded of this at regular intervals. Irreverence irritates leaders but is their salvation. Unquestioning submission corrupts leaders and demeans followers. Making a cult of a leader is always a mistake. Fortunately, hero worship generates its own antidote. "Every hero," said Emerson, "becomes a bore at last."

The signal benefit the great leaders confer is to embolden the rest of us to live according to our own best selves, to be active, insistent, and resolute in affirming our own sense of things. For great leaders attest to the reality of human freedom against the supposed inevitabilities of history. And they attest to the wisdom and power that may lie within the most unlikely of us, which is why Abraham Lincoln remains the supreme example of great leadership. A great leader, said Emerson, exhibits new possibilities to all humanity. "We feed on genius. . . . Great men exist that there may be greater men."

Great leaders, in short, justify themselves by emancipating and empowering their followers. So humanity struggles to master its destiny, remembering with Alexis de Tocqueville: "It is true that around every man a fatal circle is traced beyond which he cannot pass; but within the wide verge of that circle he is powerful and free; as it is with man, so with communities." ◆

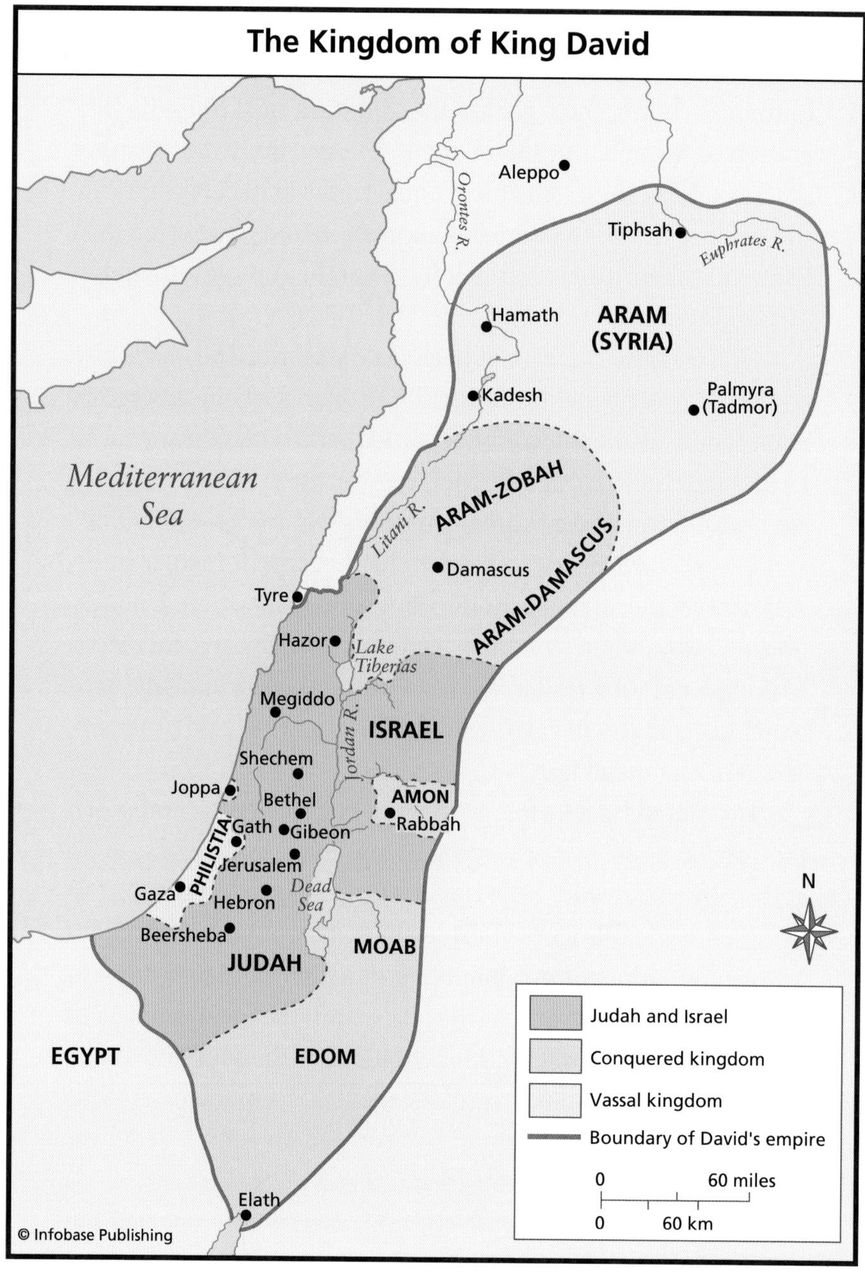
The Kingdom of King David
Aleppo
Orontes R.
Tiphsah
Euphrates R.
Hamath
ARAM (SYRIA)
Kadesh
Palmyra (Tadmor)
Mediterranean Sea
ARAM-ZOBAH
Litani R.
ARAM-DAMASCUS
Damascus
Tyre
Hazor
Lake Tiberias
Megiddo
Jordan R.
ISRAEL
Shechem
Joppa
Bethel
AMON
Rabbah
Gath
Gibeon
PHILISTIA
Jerusalem
Gaza
Hebron
Dead Sea
Beersheba
MOAB
JUDAH
EGYPT
EDOM
Elath
N
Judah and Israel
Conquered kingdom
Vassal kingdom
Boundary of David's empire
0 60 miles
0 60 km
© Infobase Publishing

CHAPTER

1

Who Was King David?

THREE THOUSAND YEARS AFTER HIS DEATH, KING DAVID REMAINS ONE of the best-known and admired leaders of the ancient world. The subject of countless literary, scholarly, and artistic works, including Michelangelo's famous marble sculpture, David is generally believed to have ruled the kingdom of Israel for nearly half a century during the late 1000s and early 900s B.C. According to the Bible, David rose from humble beginnings as a sheepherder to become a mighty warrior-king and founder of an empire that included not only the modern state of Israel but also parts of present-day Jordan, Syria, and Lebanon.

Over the millennia, the Hebrew Bible (the Old Testament to Christians) and especially its books of Samuel, Kings, and Chronicles have been the chief source for David's life.

Exceptionally devout and brave yet capable of great cruelty and selfishness, David is not only one of the most fascinating figures in the Hebrew Scriptures but also the most mentioned. His name appears in the Bible over 1,000 times, 300 more times than the next most mentioned person, the Hebrew patriarch Moses.

ARCHAEOLOGICAL EVIDENCE FOR THE LIFE OF DAVID

Aside from the biblical books of Samuel, Kings, and Chronicles, several recent archaeological discoveries have offered new—if limited—information about David. The first of these findings came to light in 1993 when a stele, an inscribed upright slab or stone, was found at the site of the ancient town of Tel Dan in northern Israel. Dating to the mid-800s B.C., about a century after David is thought to have died, the Tel Dan Stele provided the first nonbiblical evidence of David's existence. Erected by a king from what is today Syria, the stele refers to the death of a Hebrew prince from "the House [dynasty or ruling family] of David."

Another possible mention of King David from ancient times was identified during the late 1990s by a scholar studying an inscription on the wall of the Temple of Amun in Karnak, Egypt. The inscription, which dates to the 900s B.C., may refer to a place in southernmost Israel called the "highland" or "heights of David." The rugged and remote southern reaches of Israel are closely linked with David in the Bible. According to the Scriptures, before claiming the throne, David spent years hiding out in the wilderness of southern Israel from his jealous predecessor, King Saul.

THE DEBATE OVER DAVID

Over the years, archaeologists have unsuccessfully sought clues regarding the life and reign of King David in Jerusalem, the city identified in the Bible as his royal capital. Because Jerusalem

First discovered by archaeologists in northernmost Israel in 1993, the Tel Dan Stele *(above)* dates back to the mid-ninth century B.C., about a century after King David is believed to have died. A reference in the stele to the "House [dynasty] of David" caused a sensation among the scholarly community because it marked the first mention of David outside of the Bible.

has been destroyed and rebuilt repeatedly over the past several thousand years, locating archaeological evidence there from as far back as the tenth and eleventh centuries B.C. has proven extremely difficult. Yet in 2005, Israeli archaeologist Dr. Eilat Mazar made a stunning announcement: She had discovered pottery dating to David's time within the remains of what was clearly a large public building in Jerusalem's oldest section. Mazar is convinced that she has unearthed David's palace, which is briefly described in the First Book of Samuel. Other archaeologists, however, remain skeptical regarding the true purpose of the ancient structure Mazar uncovered, and more excavating will need to be done before her theory about the building can be proved.

The discovery of the Tel Dan Stele, the interpretation of the inscription at Egypt's Temple of Amun, and most recently, Dr. Mazar's dramatic claim to have found King David's palace, have brought renewed attention to a longstanding debate about David. Before the Tel Dan discovery, some scholars questioned whether David had ever lived at all, arguing that he may have been no more than a legendary hero, the Israelites' version of England's King Arthur. Since the finding at Tel Dan, few historians or archaeologists still question the existence of a Hebrew leader named David. However, some scholars doubt whether David was as powerful and influential a ruler as the Bible reports. Until more research can be carried out in Jerusalem and elsewhere within Israel and its Middle Eastern neighbors, the debate over exactly who King David was and what he did or did not accomplish will undoubtedly continue.

CHAPTER

2

"We Want a King"

MOST SCHOLARS BELIEVE THAT KING DAVID WAS BORN IN THE TOWN OF Bethlehem, in what is today the Palestinian-controlled territory of the West Bank, sometime during the eleventh century B.C., possibly around 1040 B.C. At the time of David's birth, Bethlehem was inhabited by an ancient people called the Hebrews, the ancestors of the Jews. The Hebrews were also referred to as Israelites in honor of their traditional patriarch Jacob, or Israel (Hebrew for "God prevails"). According to the Hebrew Scriptures, Israel's many sons founded and lent their names to the Twelve Tribes of Israel: Reuben, Levi, Simeon, Issachar, Zebulun, Dan, Judah, Gad, Asher, Naphtali, Joseph, and Benjamin. David and his family—like most residents of Bethlehem—belonged to the large and powerful tribe of Judah.

DAVID'S HEBREW ANCESTORS

In about 1800 B.C., David's Hebrew ancestors may have first settled in the narrow strip of land that today includes the State of Israel and the territories of the Palestinian Authority. According to the Scriptures, the Jews' first patriarch, Israel's grandfather Abraham, guided the Hebrew people out of Mesopotamia, the ancient region between the two great Middle Eastern rivers, the Tigris and the Euphrates. Abraham led the Hebrews to Canaan—an area that encompasses Israel and the Palestinian Authority territories as well as parts of Jordan, Syria, and Lebanon. Abraham and his flock, the Bible relates, had migrated to Canaan on the command of their god, Yahweh: "Go from your country and your kindred and your father's house to the land that I will show you," Yahweh ordered Abraham. "I will make of you a great nation, and I will bless you. . . ." (Genesis 12:1–2).

Yahweh, the Scriptures report, promised "all the land of Canaan" to his "Chosen People," the Hebrews, and their descendants in exchange for their obedience (Genesis 17:8). Nonetheless, Canaan was not an empty land when the Hebrews arrived. A number of different ethnic groups already lived there, peoples who are often lumped together under the label of Canaanite. The majority of the Hebrew immigrants settled in one of the most thinly populated sections of the region—the rocky hill country that lay between Canaan's fertile coastal plains and the Jordan River. The early Hebrews appear to have been mostly sheepherders and goatherds, although they may also have been part-time farmers.

Just two centuries after the Hebrews migrated to central Canaan, in about 1600 B.C., a terrible famine struck the region, the Bible reports. Faced with starvation, the Hebrews fled their Promised Land, journeying southward toward the rich and powerful North African kingdom of Egypt. But abandoning Canaan for Egypt turned out to be a serious mistake. The vast kingdom's supreme rulers, the pharaohs, distrusted the Hebrew refugees and eventually enslaved them. According to the Scriptures, after four centuries of bondage, the Israelites finally made their exodus, or flight, from Egypt under the guidance of a devout new leader, Moses, and set off on the long journey back toward Canaan.

While Moses was shepherding his charges across the Sinai Desert toward Canaan, Yahweh revealed to him the Ten Commandments—the core spiritual and moral duties of the Hebrews to God and their fellow humans. According to the Bible, the first and most important of Moses' laws stated: "I am the Lord your God, . . . you shall have no other gods before me" (Exodus 20:2–3). The Hebrews' insistence that there was just one deity, or god—a form of religious belief known as monotheism—made them unique among the ancient peoples of the Middle East. All of the Hebrews' neighbors were polytheists, meaning that they worshipped many different gods.

During their long and difficult trek across the Sinai, Moses' flock became discouraged and wanted to turn back to Egypt. The Hebrews' faltering faith angered Yahweh, who had promised to deliver them safely to their Promised Land. As punishment for their lack of faith, God caused the Israelites to wander aimlessly for four decades in the desert wilderness, the Bible reports. At last, around 1200 B.C., the Hebrews found their way back to central Canaan under the leadership of Moses' right-hand man, Joshua. Over the course of the next 100 years or so, they would succeed in absorbing or subduing most of the other inhabitants of the region.

"IN THOSE DAYS THERE WAS NO KING IN ISRAEL"

By the time of David's birth about the mid-eleventh century B.C., however, the Israelites faced new challenges for control of their Promised Land. The most serious challenge to Israelite rule in central Canaan came from the mighty Philistines. A seafaring people, the Philistines probably voyaged to Canaan from the Aegean, an arm of the Mediterranean Sea between Turkey and Greece. After arriving in Canaan, the Philistines soon founded several large cities and trading centers near the Mediterranean, to the southwest of Bethlehem. Wealthier and more technologically advanced than the Israelites, most of whom were small herders or farmers, the Philistines quickly assembled a large, well-equipped army. Then they began pushing ever farther eastward from their coastal strongholds into Hebrew territory.

During the first half of the eleventh century B.C., in contrast to most of their neighbors—including the Egyptians, the Philistines, and the Moabites and Ammonites, two ancient peoples from what is now western Jordan—the Israelites were not ruled by a king. "In those days there was no king in Israel; all the people did what was right in their own eyes," the Bible relates (Judges 21:25). While their neighbors in west Asia and North Africa had progressed from tribal rule to strong, centralized monarchies, the Israelites continued to organize themselves into a loose union of tribes based on the traditional Twelve Tribes of their patriarch Israel.

Each of the Twelve Tribes was headed by a council of elders, who made decisions that affected the welfare of the entire group. To help settle the inevitable arguments that arose between neighboring tribes, interpret Moses' law, and create an intertribal militia during times of war, the Israelites also gradually developed the position of "judge." Hebrew judges were almost always well-known and respected religious figures. The one and only female judge, Deborah, was a prophet, meaning that she was supposedly the medium through which Yahweh spoke to his people. According to Hebrew tradition, prophets were also supposed to inspire Yahweh's followers to repent of their sins and honor his commandments. Samuel, the last of the Hebrew judges, was also the Israelites' chief prophet and high priest during David's early years. Despite his high standing as a spiritual leader, however, Samuel had no way of guaranteeing that his decisions would be followed throughout the Promised Land. The various tribes were not under any formal obligation to heed

After the escape from Egypt, Moses led the Israelites into the Sinai Desert. According to the scriptures, God revealed the Ten Commandments to Moses while he was guiding the Israelites across the Sinai toward Canaan. Although there is no archaeological proof Moses and his people wandered this desert for 40 years, researchers are beginning to discover evidence proving the existence of famous biblical figures like King David.

a judge's orders. Therefore, the control—judicial, administrative, or military—that Samuel could actually exercise over the Israelites was strictly limited.

Deborah, Judge and Prophet

The judge and prophet Deborah has been called the greatest female figure in the Hebrew Scriptures. Most women in the Bible are mentioned only within the context of their relationships to important men—as their wives, daughters, sisters, or mothers. Deborah is an exception to that rule. The only woman in ancient Israel to hold the office of judge, Deborah "used to sit under the palm of Deborah . . . in the hill country of Ephraim and the Israelites came up to her for judgment," the Scriptures relate (Judges 4:5).

Deborah is believed to have lived about a century after the Israelites returned to Canaan from Egypt. At that time, the valley where she lived in northern Israel was under the control of a tyrannical Canaanite ruler, King Jabin. According to the Book of Judges, Deborah appointed a Hebrew warrior named Barak to take 10,000 men and confront King Jabin's commander Sisera and his formidable force, which included 900 iron-trimmed chariots, on Mount Tabor. The Israelites, who did not even possess the technology to make iron, had no chariots, iron trimmed or otherwise. Their army was made up entirely of foot soldiers. Deborah's role as her people's most trusted religious and political leader is evident in Barak's response to the judge-prophet: "If you will go with me, I will go; but if you will not go with me, I will not go" (Judges 4:8).

Deborah, Barak, and their army then set out bravely for Mount Tabor. Happily for the Israelites, it was the rainy season and the battlefield was covered with a thick layer of mud. Sisera's 900 chariots quickly became bogged down in the mire and the Israelites were able to defeat the enemy army, despite the Canaanites' technological superiority. The famous poem, the "Song of Deborah" found in the fifth chapter of the Book of Judges, celebrates the Israelite victory on Mount Tabor and is considered one of the oldest surviving examples of Hebrew literature.

"GIVE US A KING"

Given the traditionally independent spirit of the Twelve Tribes and their elders, the Israelites had managed to live quite contentedly for centuries without a strong, centralized political authority. Yet the growing Philistine threat in their own backyard during the eleventh century B.C. caused many Israelites to change their minds regarding the best form of government. According to the Bible, sometime around 1030 B.C., when David was probably still a child, a group of tribal leaders approached Samuel with a heartfelt request: "Give us a king to govern us," they cried (1 Samuel 8:6). Ask Yahweh to grant us a monarch at once, the elders urged, a warrior-king who would protect the Chosen People from their enemies and rule over all the tribes in God's name.

At first, the Bible reports, Samuel resisted the elders' demands, convinced that their desire for a king showed a sad lack of faith in the saving power of Yahweh and his special bond with the Israelites. Moreover, Samuel had a deep-seated prejudice against monarchies, which he saw as corrupt and self-serving. The Israelites, he cautioned the tribal leaders, stood to lose a great deal if they permitted themselves to fall under the sway of a king:

> These will be the ways of the king who will reign over you: he will take your sons and appoint them to his chariots and to be his horsemen, and to run before his chariots; and he will appoint for himself commanders of thousands and commanders of fifties, and some to plow his ground and to reap his harvest, and to make his implements of war and the equipment of his chariots. He will take your daughters to be perfumers and cooks and bakers. He will take the best of your fields and vineyards and olive orchards and give them to his courtiers. . . . He will take your male and female slaves, and the best of your cattle and donkeys, and put them to his

> work. He will take one-tenth of your flocks, and you shall be his slaves. And in that day you will cry out because of your king, whom you have chosen for yourselves; but the Lord will not answer you in that day (1 Samuel 8:11–18).

To Samuel's dismay, the elders brushed off his warnings regarding the pitfalls of monarchies. They were so frightened of their warlike neighbors that they were ready to take the risk that their king-commander might turn out to be grasping and power hungry. "We are determined to have a king over us, so that we also may be like other nations, and that our king may govern us and go out before us and fight our battles," the elders insisted (1 Samuel 8:19–20). Samuel realized that he had no choice but to give in to the tribal leaders' demands. The Israelites shall have their king, he proclaimed; however, he added, the new ruler had to be appointed by the Lord God himself, who would divulge the chosen one's identity to his prophet, Samuel.

THE ANOINTING OF KING SAUL

Yahweh, the Bible relates, did not at first reveal to Samuel the king's name but only that he would be from the tribe of Benjamin. This probably made sense to Samuel because although the tribe of Benjamin was the smallest of the Twelve Tribes, its members were renown throughout Canaan for their courage and military skill. Soon after receiving the message that the Israelites' first king was to be a Benjaminite, Samuel was introduced to Saul, a handsome farmer from that tribe who lived in the town of Gibeah, not far from Bethlehem. An experienced fighter, Samuel had a reputation for extraordinary bravery on the battlefield, even by the lofty standards of his warlike tribe. Standing a full head taller than the average man, Saul certainly looked like a king. Samuel quickly concluded that he was the Benjaminite whom God had appointed to rule over the Hebrews.

Within 24 hours of meeting Saul, Samuel formally anointed him as the Israelites' first king. For the ancient Hebrews, anointing a person's head with oil was an important symbolic gesture. It signified that the anointed one—whether priest, prophet, or political leader—had devoted himself to the service of Yahweh and, in return, would be blessed with heavenly wisdom and strength. In contrast to most of their neighbors in the Middle East and North Africa, however, the Hebrews did not look on their king as divine or godlike. Instead, they viewed him as fully human and therefore subject to the same moral and religious laws as any other member of the community.

Soon after the private anointing ceremony, Samuel called the leaders of the Twelve Tribes to a special assembly and introduced them to Saul. The elders greeted their new ruler enthusiastically. Accompanied by a large following of advisors and warriors from his tribe, Saul returned to his hometown of Gibeah, where he planned to establish the royal capital. So began what is known in the history of the Israelites as the United Monarchy period, when the 12 Hebrew tribes agreed to submit to the authority of a single king.

SAUL RAISES AN ARMY

According to the Bible, Saul's chief task as king of Israel was revealed to Samuel by the Lord himself right before he met the Benjaminite for the first time: the king shall deliver God's people from their enemies, Yahweh told Samuel, "for I have seen the suffering of my people" (1 Samuel 9:16). Soon after taking the throne, Saul's commitment to protecting God's Chosen People was put to the test when the Hebrew frontier town of Jabesh-Gilead was besieged by a large Ammonite army. The townspeople sent a frantic message to Ammon's king, Nahash, offering to accept his rule if he would only abandon the siege. But Nahash treated the Israelites' plea for mercy with contempt:

"On this condition I will make a treaty with you," he sneered, "namely that I gouge out everyone's right eye, and thus put disgrace upon all Israel" (1 Samuel 11:2). The terrified inhabitants of Jabesh-Gilead asked for seven days to make a decision regarding the king's cruel offer, then hastily sent out a message to Saul begging for his help.

Incensed by Nahash's humiliating and brutal attitude toward his subjects, Saul resolved to raise a national army to rescue the citizens of Jabesh-Gilead. To ensure that the independent-minded Israelites heeded his call to arms, Saul decided to rely on strong-arm tactics in mobilizing his army. "He took a yoke [pair] of oxen," the Bible relates, "and cut them in pieces and sent them throughout all the territory of Israel by messengers, saying, 'Whoever does not come out after Saul and Samuel, so shall it be done to his oxen!' " Saul's strategy worked: "The dread of the Lord fell upon the people," the Bible says, "and they came out as one" (1 Samuel 11:7). Having assembled an army of more than 300,000 men, Saul was able to launch a devastating attack on the Ammonite camp near Jabesh-Gilead, scattering Nahash's troops and ending his kingdom's threat to Israel, at least for the time being.

SAUL'S DISOBEDIENCE AT MICHMASH

Although Saul had for all intents and purposes coerced the Israelites into joining his new army, following their victory over the Ammonites, they treated their new king as a national hero and deliverer. Encouraged by Saul's widespread support, the king's eldest son and heir, Prince Jonathan, decided the time was ripe to attack Israel's chief rivals in Canaan, the Philistines. Acting on his own initiative, Jonathan led a daring and bloody ambush on a Philistine regiment. The incensed Philistines quickly vowed revenge. Realizing that a full-scale military conflict was inevitable, Saul fired off a message to his high priest, Samuel. In the letter Saul asked Samuel to come

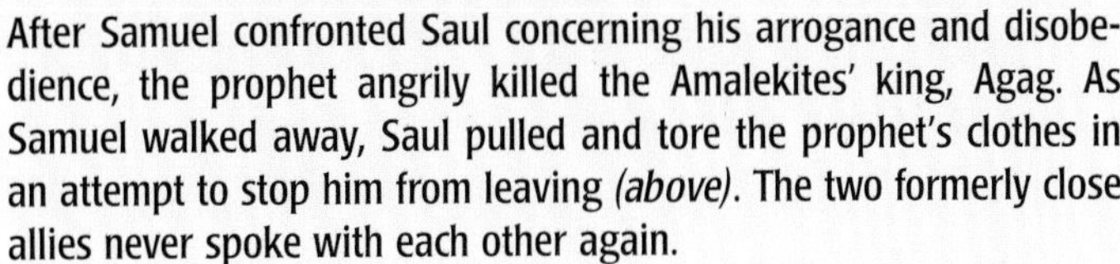

After Samuel confronted Saul concerning his arrogance and disobedience, the prophet angrily killed the Amalekites' king, Agag. As Samuel walked away, Saul pulled and tore the prophet's clothes in an attempt to stop him from leaving *(above)*. The two formerly close allies never spoke with each other again.

to the town of Michmash, where he was mustering his army, to carry out the customary war sacrifice of a young oxen or lamb. Like most of their neighbors in Canaan, the followers of Yahweh sought to please their deity and win his favor through the gift of sacrifice—the ritual slaughter of an animal or animals.

Samuel sent back word that he would meet the king in seven days to make the traditional burnt offering to Yahweh. But when the old man failed to show up at Michmash exactly on time, Saul became impatient and decided to make the sacrifice himself. The war against the Philistines ultimately resulted in victory for Saul and his troops. But Samuel, who arrived at Michmash just as the sacrificial animals were going up in flame, was deeply offended by the king's unwillingness to wait for his guidance in carrying out the solemn rite. Convinced that Saul had greatly overstepped his authority by performing what had always been a priestly responsibility—the making of burnt offerings—Samuel scolded Saul for his arrogance. Not only were his days as king of Israel numbered, the prophet predicted, but neither Jonathan nor any of Saul's other descendents would inherit his throne. Instead, the crown would go to another Israelite, a man after the Lord's "own heart." Samuel prophesized: "The Lord would have established your kingdom over Israel forever, but now your kingdom will not continue; the Lord has sought out a man after his own heart; and the Lord has appointed him to be ruler over his people, because you have not kept what the Lord has commanded you" (1 Samuel 13:13–14).

SAMUEL VERSUS SAUL: "YOU HAVE REJECTED THE WORD OF THE LORD"

Despite the priest's dire prediction, however, over the next several months Saul continued to enjoy victories against the Israelites' enemies, including the neighboring kingdoms of Moab and Edom. With each victory on the battlefield, the king only seemed to become more arrogant and reckless. Finally, after Saul delivered a stinging defeat to the Israelites' longtime enemies, the Amalekites, a nomadic people who lived in what is today southern Israel and the Sinai Peninsula, Samuel lost all patience with the headstrong monarch. Before Saul launched his war against the Amalekites, Samuel had specifically directed the king to slaughter every Amalekite man, woman, and child he could get his hands on, along with all of their livestock. Samuel insisted that Yahweh wanted the Amalekite people utterly destroyed because of their many past cruelties to his Chosen People, cruelties that dated all the way back to Moses' time. Instead of obeying the high priest, however, Samuel quietly saved the best of the Amalekites' sheep and cattle, perhaps to share out to his troops as booty (a prize of battle). Saul also decided to spare the life of the Amalekite king, Agag.

When Samuel paid a surprise visit to Saul to confront him with his disobedience, Saul tried to mollify the old priest by promising to sacrifice the Amalekites' sheep and cattle as a burnt offering to Yahweh. But Samuel was unbending. "You have rejected the word of the Lord, and the Lord has rejected you from being king over Israel," he coldly informed Saul (1 Samuel 15:26). Then grabbing a sword, the priest ran Agag through and headed for the door without another word. As he passed by, Saul seized the prophet's arm to stop him, accidentally tearing Samuel's robe in the process. Just so, Samuel responded, would Yahweh tear away the kingdom of Israel from his wayward servant Saul and give it to another. With that, Samuel turned his back on Saul and left. The king and the priest who had anointed him would never see each other again. Soon after the final rift between Saul and Samuel, the Bible relates, God sent an evil spirit to torment the king. Although he would keep his crown for many more years, both Saul's fortunes and his mental health began a steady decline from that time onward.

CHAPTER

3

"This Is the One"

SOON AFTER SAMUEL SAID GOOD-BYE TO KING SAUL FOR GOOD, THE BIBLE relates, Yahweh sent the elderly priest on a mission to find and anoint a new ruler for the Israelites. "Fill your horn with oil and set out," Yahweh ordered. "I am sending you to Jesse the Bethlehemite, for I have provided for myself a king among his sons." But Samuel was reluctant to follow God's command. Saul would surely have him killed if the king found out about his mission, the prophet complained to Yahweh. "Bring a heifer [a young cow] along with you," God replied, "and say, I have come to sacrifice for the Lord. Invite Jesse to the sacrifice, and I will show you what you shall do; and you shall anoint for me the one whom I name to you" (1 Samuel 16:1–3).

THE SONS OF JESSE

So Samuel, heifer in tow, set off from his hometown of Ramah for Bethlehem, a journey of some 10 miles. He soon located the house of Jesse, a farmer and herder and the father of a large brood, including eight sons and at least two daughters. Careful not to reveal his true mission in Bethlehem, Samuel invited Jesse and his family to attend a ritual sacrifice to Yahweh. Then he asked Jesse to introduce him to each of his sons. When the eldest, a tall and muscular young man named Eliab, was brought before him, Samuel thought:

> 'Surely the Lord's anointed is now before the Lord.' But the Lord said to Samuel, 'Do not look on his appearance or on the height of his stature, because I have rejected him; for the Lord does not see as mortals see; they look on the outward appearance, but the Lord looks in the heart.' Then Jesse called Abinadab, and made him pass before Samuel. He said, 'Neither has the Lord chosen this one.' Jesse made seven of his sons pass before Samuel, and Samuel said to Jesse, 'The Lord has not chosen any of these. . . . Are all your sons here?' (1 Samuel 16:6–11)

In fact, Jesse had neglected to call his last son, David, home to greet the prophet. The youngest male in the family, David had been assigned the humble task of watching Jesse's sheep. As usual, he was off somewhere with the flock on the grassy slopes above Bethlehem. Samuel immediately told Jesse to send for the boy. When the missing son—a handsome boy of 16 or 17, although not tall like his brother Eliab—arrived, Yahweh ordered the prophet to "rise and anoint him; for this is the one," the Bible relates (1 Samuel 6:12). With only David's father and seven brothers as witnesses, Samuel anointed the teenager by pouring oil on his head, probably olive oil mixed with sweet smelling spices. It is unclear from the scriptural account whether any of those present—including David himself—really understood what Samuel's dramatic gesture meant. As soon as the priest departed, David promptly returned to his shepherding duties and his family seems to have treated him no differently than before.

KING SAUL'S NEW MINSTREL

In the meantime, Saul's mental health was steadily deteriorating. Many modern scholars have concluded that the king suffered from some form of mental illness, such as severe depression or anxiety. Yet, like most of his fellow Israelites, Saul blamed his psychological distress on "evil spirits" instead of a mental disorder. If he had any hope of driving away the malicious spirits that tormented him, Saul believed, he would have to have expert assistance. The king therefore called his courtiers and servants together and commanded them to hunt down not a doctor or a priest, as might be expected, but rather a minstrel. In his book *King David: A Biography*, biblical scholar Steven McKenzie explains: "Saul did not want music for entertainment. In the ancient world, music served more of a religious and magical foundation. . . . Music was believed to possess magical powers to keep away or exorcise demons and evil spirits."

It happened that one of Saul's attendants had heard reports of a skilled musician who lived just a few miles from the capital city of Gibeah, in the Judahite town of Bethlehem. His name, the man informed the king, was David, and he was the youngest son of Jesse. Saul, who had no inkling of the connection between David and Samuel, immediately sent a message to Bethlehem commanding the teenager to come to the royal residence. Jesse dutifully loaded up a donkey with gifts for Saul—loaves of bread, wine, and a young goat—and sent them along with David to Gibeah.

When David performed for Saul, the king discovered that the boy was not only a gifted singer and songwriter but also a talented lyre player. Widely believed to have been invented in

On a mission to find the new leader of Israel, Samuel met Jesse's seven oldest sons but did not choose any of them. When Jesse finally presented his youngest son, David, to Samuel, God immediately informed the prophet "this is the one" and Samuel anointed the teenager as the Israelites' king.

about 3200 B.C. by the Sumerians, an ancient people of southern Mesopotamia, the lyre is a stringed instrument that looks something like a small harp. Lyres of the sort that David probably would have owned featured a hollow wooden sound box, usually trapezoidal in shape. Extending up from the sound box were two gracefully curved arms of unequal length, with the shorter arm held next to the musician. The arms were joined near the top by a crossbar or yoke from which were stretched 8 to 10 long strings made of sheep gut. Of varying thickness, the strings were plucked with the fingers or with a plectrum, a type of slender pick.

David's music, and particularly his lyre playing, soothed King Saul's frazzled nerves as nothing else had. Whenever an evil spirit "came upon Saul," the Bible relates, "David took the lyre and played it with his hand, and Saul would be relieved and feel better, and the evil spirit would depart from him" (1 Samuel 16: 23). David quickly became a special favorite of the king. Saul even allowed the teenager to serve as his personal armor-bearer, a distinct honor for the youngest son of a Bethlehem farmer.

GOLIATH OF GATH

According to the Bible, Saul gave David permission to travel home now and then to visit his family and help Jesse with the sheep. During one of the teenager's visits in Bethlehem, the off again, on again conflict between the Israelites and their neighbors, the Philistines, heated up once more. Three of David's older brothers had recently joined Saul's army, which was currently in a standoff with a large Philistine force deep within Israelite territory on the slopes of the Valley of Elah. The Hebrew army had congregated on the north side of the valley, and the Philistine force had massed directly across from them on the south. As the stalemate dragged on, Jesse worried that the army would run out of provisions. Since Elah was less than a day's walk from Bethlehem, he decided to send David to Saul's camp with loaves of bread and other food from home for his three brothers.

Soon after David arrived at Saul's encampment, the enemy's most powerful warrior, an enormous man from the city of Goth by the name of Goliath, boldly stepped forth from the Philistine lines and shouted out a challenge to the Israelites. "Why have you come out to draw up for battle?" he sneered. "Choose a man for yourselves, and let him come down to me. If he is able to fight with me and kill me, then we will be your servants; but if I prevail against him and kill him, then you shall be our servants and serve us" (1 Samuel 17:8–9). But not a single Israelite soldier volunteered to take Goliath up on his offer of a one-on-one, winner-take-all fight.

In truth, the Israelites were scared to death of the Philistine warrior. According to the Bible, Goliath in his full battle regalia was an awe-inspiring sight. Encased in metal from head to foot, Goliath sported a bronze helmet, plated body armor, and greaves (shin guards) that together weighed well over 100 pounds. He carried a curved bronze sword, a javelin, and a huge spear with a shaft as heavy and broad "as a weaver's beam," the Scriptures further relate, and a shield-bearer walked before him (1 Samuel 17:7).

Perhaps even more intimidating to the Israelites than Goliath's armor and weaponry was the Philistine's massive size. Goliath, the Bible's First Book of Samuel maintains, was a bona fide giant who stood "six cubits and a span" tall (1 Samuel 17:4). Cubits and spans were ancient units of measurement based on the human body. A cubit was equivalent to the approximate length of an adult forearm and a span to the width of an open adult hand. Since a cubit equals about one and a half feet and a span about nine inches, that would have made Goliath an astounding nine and three-quarters feet tall! Scholars believe that this startling figure was significantly inflated over time, however. During the mid-twentieth century, an older copy of the First Book of Samuel that portrays Goliath as much smaller was discovered among the famous Dead Sea Scrolls. These ancient papyrus and leather scrolls containing passages from the Hebrew Scriptures were found during the 1940s and 1950s in caves along the Dead Sea, near the border between modern Jordan and Israel. According to the Dead Sea Scroll version of the well-known biblical story, Goliath's height was just four cubits and a span—about six feet nine inches. By modern standards, a man six and three-quarters feet tall would probably not be considered a giant. Nonetheless, scientific evidence suggests that the average person was considerably shorter in ancient times. Thus, whether he measured six cubits and a span or four cubits and a span from head to toe, Goliath still would have appeared extraordinarily large to his frightened opponents at the Valley of Elah.

FAITH AND COURAGE

As Goliath continued to call out his challenge to the Israelites, young David was listening closely from the Israelites' side of the valley. He considered Goliath's arrogant attitude toward Saul's troops as a reproach against not only his homeland and king, but also his god. "For who is this uncircumcised Philistine that he should defy the armies of the living God?" David angrily demanded of a group of soldiers standing next to him on the hillside (1 Samuel 17:26). According to the Bible, David also displayed a deep interest in the generous reward Saul had promised to anyone who managed to kill the giant. Goliath's slayer, the king had promised his troops, would receive great riches and his entire household would be exempt from all government taxes. Clearly persuaded that he would be furthering God's cause as well as his own by fighting the Philistine, David resolved to go to the king's tent and inform him that he would take Goliath up on his challenge.

Saul, the Bible reports, was clearly taken aback by the teenager's brave offer. "You are just a boy," he gently reminded David, "and he has been a warrior from his youth" (1 Samuel 17:33). While it was true that he was only a humble shepherd boy, David replied, more than once he had had to rescue his father's flock from vicious predators, including a lion and a bear. Now he was ready and willing to rescue God's Hebrew flock from the savage Philistines. "The Lord, who saved me from the paw of the lion and from the paw of the bear, will save me from the hand of this Philistine," David assured the king (1 Samuel 17:37).

Reluctantly, Saul gave his favorite minstrel his blessing. Then, in a gesture that highlighted his affection for the teenager, he dressed David in his own armor. Significantly smaller than Saul, David found the king's armor too heavy and awkward, however, and quickly removed it. Wearing his everyday clothing and armed merely with a shepherd's staff or stick and a leather slingshot, David headed off to meet Goliath. "Go," Saul said

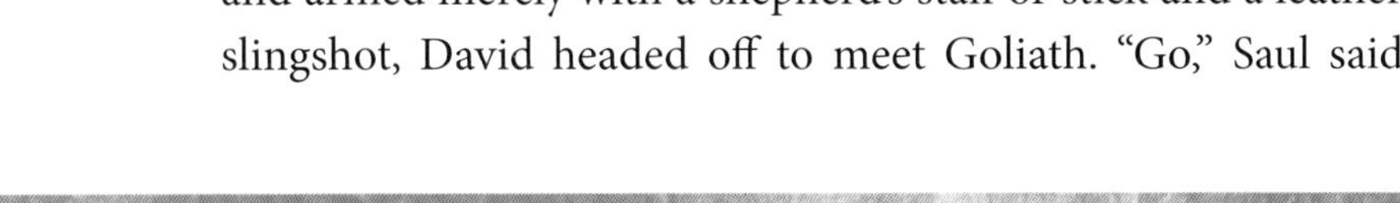

The Dead Sea Scrolls

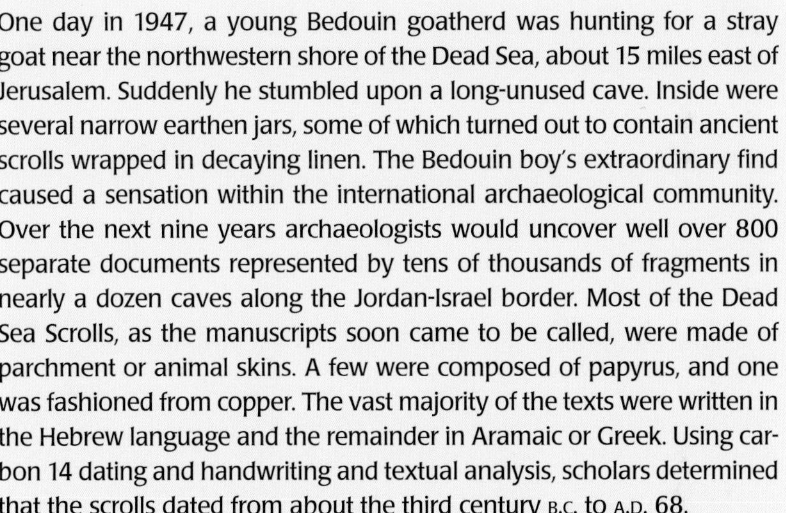

One day in 1947, a young Bedouin goatherd was hunting for a stray goat near the northwestern shore of the Dead Sea, about 15 miles east of Jerusalem. Suddenly he stumbled upon a long-unused cave. Inside were several narrow earthen jars, some of which turned out to contain ancient scrolls wrapped in decaying linen. The Bedouin boy's extraordinary find caused a sensation within the international archaeological community. Over the next nine years archaeologists would uncover well over 800 separate documents represented by tens of thousands of fragments in nearly a dozen caves along the Jordan-Israel border. Most of the Dead Sea Scrolls, as the manuscripts soon came to be called, were made of parchment or animal skins. A few were composed of papyrus, and one was fashioned from copper. The vast majority of the texts were written in the Hebrew language and the remainder in Aramaic or Greek. Using carbon 14 dating and handwriting and textual analysis, scholars determined that the scrolls dated from about the third century B.C. to A.D. 68.

About a third of the Dead Sea texts are from the Hebrew Scriptures, including fragments from every book of the Old Testament except the Book of Esther. The historic and religious significance of these fragments is enormous since they are nearly 1,000 years older than any other surviving texts of the Hebrew Bible. The remaining Dead Sea Scrolls include traditional Hebrew religious writings that are not part of the Bible, such as the Book of Jubilees, the Testament of Levi, and the Book of Enoch; biblical commentaries; hymns; prayers; and various texts that appear to represent the beliefs of a Jewish sect that probably lived near the caves. Some scholars believe that all the scrolls belonged to this sect and were hidden in the caves in about A.D. 70 during the First Jewish Revolt against the Romans.

simply to the young warrior, "and may the Lord be with you!" (1 Samuel 17:37).

THE GIANT AND THE SHEPHERD BOY

When Goliath caught sight of the "champion" the Israelites had sent to fight him, he was disdainful. Pointing to David's wooden staff, he jeered, "Am I a dog, that you come to me with sticks? . . . Come to me, and I will give your flesh to the birds of the air and to the wild animals of the field." But David, confident in the belief that he was doing the Lord's work and the Heavenly Father would protect him, was not afraid: "You come to me with sword and spear and javelin," David boldly told Goliath,

> but I come to you in the name of the Lord of hosts, the God of the armies of Israel, whom you have defied. This very day the Lord will deliver you into my hand, and I will strike you down and cut off your hand; and I will give the dead bodies of the Philistine army this very day to the birds of the air and to the animals of the earth, So that all the earth may know that there is a God in Israel; . . . for the battle is the Lord's and he will give you into our hand. (1 Samuel 17:43–47)

Goliath, weighed down by his bulky armor, began lumbering down the hillside toward David. Suddenly the teenager rushed at the Philistine, pulling his sling and a large smooth stone out of his pouch as he ran. Before Goliath probably even realized what was happening, David had loaded his sling and, aiming the weapon directly at the Philistine's forehead, let go. The hard missile struck Goliath squarely between the eyes, the one portion of his forehead that was unprotected by his helmet. A moment later the gigantic warrior toppled facedown onto the ground, dead.

To the modern reader, it may seem difficult to believe that a heavily armed soldier could be felled by a single shot from a sling. But the sling of David's time was no child's toy. Rather it was a fearsome weapon widely prized throughout the Middle East and Europe for its effectiveness. Indeed, some of the most

Offended by Goliath's brazen attitude in challenging God's Chosen People, David volunteered to fight in a one-on-one battle with the Philistine giant. Although the Israelites, including King Saul, were reluctant to send the young sheepherder, David proved them wrong and killed Goliath. The Philistines ran away in fear and shock after seeing David holding Goliath's head *(above)*.

powerful armies of the ancient world actually preferred the sling to the bow and arrow in combat. "The slinger was more mobile than the archer, and with a greater accurate range, some say with a more damaging projectile," writes author Robert Pinsky in *The Life of David*. "The Romans," Pinksy notes, "had medical tongs designed specifically for removing the stones or lead bullets shot by sling to penetrate a soldier's body, as David's stone penetrated the skull of Goliath."

As soon as David realized that he had killed Goliath, he strode over to the fallen warrior. Then, using Goliath's own sword, he chopped off his opponent's head. When the Philistine troops saw the teenager holding up the severed head of their champion, they fled the hillside in terror, with the Israelites in pursuit. Unable to overtake the retreating Philistines, the Israelites returned to their enemy's now deserted camp at Elah and plundered it. Meanwhile, back at Saul's encampment, David presented Goliath's severed head to the surprised monarch. The Philistines had been routed—at least for the time being—and the humble sheepherder from Bethlehem was hailed by the entire Israelite army as a hero.

THE CONTROVERSY OVER GOLIATH AND HIS DEATH

Unquestionably, the story of the shepherd boy David and the mighty Philistine giant he slew is one of the best-known episodes in the Bible. Yet it is also one of the most controversial. The controversy over the tale of David and Goliath centers on a puzzling passage found in the Second Book of Samuel, whose first chapters cover David's later life. In the passage from the Second Book of Samuel, a warrior by the name of Elhanan is credited with killing the giant Goliath during a battle between the Israelites and the Philistines at a place called Gob. During the battle, which took place after David had already become king of Israel, the passage relates, "Elhanan son of Jaareoregim, the Bethlehemite, killed Goliath the Gittite [meaning a native of the city of Gath], the shaft of whose spear was like a weaver's beam" (2 Samuel 21:19).

Over the years, biblical scholars have put forth several different theories to explain the apparent discrepancy between the famous version of Goliath's death found in the First Book of Samuel and the less well-known version of his death found in the Second Book of Samuel. One theory suggests that by some strange coincidence both David and Elhanan killed a giant from Gath named Goliath who carried a spear as wide and heavy as a "weaver's beam." Another theory proposes that David never killed Goliath in the first place. The story of the heroic and devout young shepherd who vanquished the giant was added to the original text years later by one of David's admirers in order to present the king in the best possible light.

A third explanation for the contradiction between the two biblical accounts is that Elhanan and David were actually one and the same person. Supporters of this theory point out that it was not uncommon for Israelite monarchs to take "throne names." For example, the birth name of King David's successor was Jedidiah, but after his coronation he changed his name to Solomon. Thus, David may have been born as Elhanan but adopted the name of David (often translated from the Hebrew as "beloved") when he took the throne. A final theory concerning the mystery of the two Goliaths argues that the account of the giant's death at the hands of Elhanan in the Second Book of Samuel is a mistake—probably the fault of a careless copyist. The real answer to the question of just who Elhanan killed in battle, this theory says, can be found in yet another book of the Bible that was written sometime after the two books of Samuel: Chronicles. "And there was again war with the Philistines; and Elhanan the son of Jair slew *Lahmi the brother of Goliath* the Gittite, the staff of whose spear was like a weaver's beam," relates verse five of the twentieth chapter of the First Book of Chronicles. (Emphasis added.)

The true explanation for the differing accounts of Goliath's death may never be known. However, it is clear from the First Book of Samuel—the chief source for David's early years—that when he was still young, David managed to distinguish himself as a courageous and skillful warrior in battle against a Philistine foe and became a national celebrity. Yet David's military success marked the beginning of a long period of conflict between the Bethlehemite and his king: As David's star rose, Saul became ever more envious and distrustful of the minstrel who had once claimed his affection and gratitude, the Bible relates. During the years ahead, Saul's growing jealousy and suspicion of David was destined to have a huge impact on both of their lives and careers.

CHAPTER

4

David and Saul

SOON AFTER DAVID'S IMPRESSIVE VICTORY AT THE VALLEY OF ELAH, KING Saul made the young warrior a commander in his army. "Wherever Saul sent him," the Bible relates, "David . . . was successful" (1 Samuel 18:5). After spending several more months harassing Philistine troops in southern and western Canaan, Saul and his men finally set off for home. It was at this point that Saul's feelings for David underwent a dramatic change from an almost fatherly affection to a deep and unreasonable hatred.

DAVID AND "HIS TEN THOUSANDS"

According to the Scriptures, the incident that triggered Saul's resentment toward the younger man took place while the army was passing through an Israelite village on their way to the royal capital at Gibeah. The women of the village rushed excitedly out of their homes to greet the king of Israel and his troops. Word of David's triumph at the Valley of Elah and his other successful campaigns against the Philistines had obviously reached their community because the women had composed a special song in honor of David and Saul. "Saul has killed his thousands," the women sang out loudly as the army marched by, "and David his ten thousands"(1 Samuel 18:7).

Saul, the Book of Samuel reports, was incensed by the villagers' ditty. How dare the women glorify a lowly commoner's accomplishments above his own, he fumed. Moreover, the king was convinced, the insulting verses hinted at treason: the villagers secretly hoped to replace him with David, the king brooded. They figured that as the superior soldier and Philistine killer, David was more deserving of the crown than Saul. "They have ascribed to David ten thousands, and to me they have ascribed thousands, what more can he have but the kingdom?" Saul wondered bitterly (1 Samuel 18:8). From that day forward Saul watched David closely. Although there is nothing in the Scriptures to indicate that David himself sought the kingship at this point in his life, as far as Saul was concerned, the young warrior from Bethlehem was his chief rival. A few years earlier at Michmash, the priest Samuel had angrily prophesized that God had already found another, more worthy ruler for Israel: "The Lord has sought out a man after his own heart; and the Lord has appointed him to be ruler over his people," Samuel had said (1 Samuel 13:13–14). That man, Saul was now convinced, was none other than David.

SAUL'S MURDEROUS PLAN

Not long after the army returned to Gibeah, the "evil spirits" that had plagued Saul ever since his final run-in with the prophet Samuel again assailed the king, and he became increasingly depressed and irritable. Unaware of the king's newfound hatred for him, Saul's servants asked David to soothe their troubled master with his lyre playing and singing, just as he had done so many times before. But when David appeared before Saul with his lyre in hand, the king was suddenly overcome by a jealous rage. Grabbing a spear, he hurled the weapon wildly at David, missing him. It is unclear from the biblical account of the episode whether David believed that Saul really meant to hurt him. He may simply have blamed the king's violent behavior on the influence of "evil spirits." At any rate, David remained at Saul's court after the incident. Soon the king, in a dramatic about-face, approached the former sheepherder with a flattering offer. If he would only agree to lead a daring new military campaign against the Philistines, the king told David, he could have the hand of Saul's eldest daughter, Merab, in marriage.

Determined to rid himself once and for all of the man he considered as his main rival, Saul had hit upon the perfect way to fulfill his murderous agenda "without bloodying his own hands," notes Jonathan Kirsch in *King David: The Real Life of the Man Who Ruled Israel*. "Even if Saul was mad [insane]," writes Kirsch, "he was also wily." First Saul promoted David to an even higher rank than he already held in the army, making him "the commander of a thousand," the Bible relates. Then the king sent the young warrior off to battle with the fervent hope that the Philistine forces would do his dirty work for him: "For Samuel thought, 'I will not raise a hand against him; let the Philistines deal with him,' " the Book of Samuel explains (1 Samuel 18:17).

The man whom the prophet Samuel had secretly anointed as Saul's successor to the throne of Israel was not to be so easily disposed of, however. To the king's dismay, David's newest military campaign against the Philistines proved a resounding success, and he soon returned to Gibeah not only very much alive but also a bigger hero to the Israelites than ever before. Nonetheless, on arriving at court David discovered that his promised reward—the hand of the king's eldest daughter in marriage—had been bestowed on another. While David was away, Saul, apparently having convinced himself that the young

Overcome by a jealous rage for the man he viewed as his chief competitor for the throne, after summoning David to play the lyre for him, Saul attempted to murder the young musician by hurling a spear at him. Despite this incident, David, apparently convinced that the king's violent action was the result of "evil spirits" rather than any deep-seated animosity toward himself, remained at Saul's court.

commander was certain to be killed, had married off Merab to Adriel the Meholathite. No one knows exactly who the "Meholathites" were, but some biblical scholars have speculated that Meholath was the name of a non-Hebrew city or district in Canaan.

DAVID AND MICHAL

At this point, one of Saul's younger daughters, Michal, confided in the king that she loved David and would be happy to wed the handsome soldier in her sister's place. Saul hastily decided that it was in his own best interest to go along with the love-struck girl: "Let me give her to him that she may be a snare for him and that the hand of the Philistines may be against him," he thought (1 Samuel 18:21). The king called David before him and informed the former shepherd that he was prepared to offer him Michal's hand in marriage—for a price.

In ancient Hebrew society a man was expected to present his fiancé's parents with a "bride price"—a valuable gift—in return for the privilege of marrying their daughter. Because David was too poor to afford a more traditional bride's gift—at least not one of the sort that a monarch might expect to receive for his daughter—Saul said David could pay his bride price to the king in battle against the Israelites' enemies. If David could kill 100 Philistines and bring back their foreskins as proof of his deed, the king promised, Saul would gladly welcome him as his new son-in-law. To Saul's delight, David promptly accepted the proposal, even though most Israelites probably would have viewed the king's grisly challenge as a suicide mission. Given the difficult and dangerous nature of the task he had assigned to David, Saul gloated, this time around his rival was almost certain to die in combat. "Beyond this story," notes biblical scholar Robert Alter in *The David Story*, "there is no indication that the Israelites had a custom of collecting the foreskins of the uncircumcised Philistines like scalps."

The Philistines

In the Bible the Philistines, the Israelites' great enemy, are presented as barbaric murderers and godless bullies. Influenced by the Scriptures' unflattering depiction of the Hebrews' chief foes in Canaan, over the centuries the word "Philistine" has come to mean an uncouth, boorish person—someone who disdains culture and learning. In recent years, however, archaeologists have uncovered an enormous amount of evidence that these immigrants to Canaan from the Aegean (an offshoot of the Mediterranean Sea between Greece and Turkey) had one of the most brilliant civilizations in the ancient Middle East.

One of the chief reasons that the Philistines posed such a formidable threat to the Israelites was their technological superiority in producing iron weapons. In contrast to the Israelites, the Philistines had many iron-making facilities throughout their territories. Consequently, their swords, spearheads, and daggers were fashioned from the exceptionally hard and durable metal. Even the Bible concedes that the Philistines of David's era were superior metalworkers who stubbornly refused to share their expertise with their neighbors, the Israelites.

Archaeological digs in eastern Israel have also revealed that the Philistines were highly advanced in terms of their artistic development. Their artisans fashioned elegant iron eating utensils and elaborately decorated pottery that contrast sharply with the plain, unpainted pottery found in Israelite towns of the same period. Excavations of Philistia's cities suggest that the Philistines were skilled architects as well, whose building designs harmoniously blended Egyptian, Aegean, and Canaanite styles.

Archaeologists believe that the standard of life in Philistine cities and towns was also relatively advanced, especially when compared to living conditions in most Israelite towns of the same period. Digs in large Philistine cities such as Ekron, on the border between Judah and Philistia, indicate that Philistine city dwellers enjoyed good sanitation facilities, running water, abundant oil lamps, and an impressive variety of cooking and other household utensils.

Yet once again, Saul had underestimated the son of Jesse. When David returned triumphantly to Gibeah with 200 Philistine foreskins—twice as many as the king had demanded for Michal's bride price—Saul had little choice but to fulfill his part of the bargain and let him wed his daughter. David's astounding success on the battlefield combined with his own child's devotion to the Bethlehemite troubled Saul enormously. Convinced that Yahweh must be firmly on the young hero's side, Saul was "more afraid of David" than ever before, the Scriptures relate, "and was David's enemy from that time forward" (1 Samuel 18:29).

DAVID AND JONATHAN

As it turned out, Michal was not the only member of the royal family who loved the man Saul had come to view as his greatest enemy. Saul's eldest son, Jonathan, was also devoted to David. Thrown together by the Israelites' ongoing war against the Philistines, the two soldiers had quickly become best friends. "The soul of Jonathan was bound to the soul of David, and Jonathan loved him as his own soul," the Bible reports (1 Samuel 18:1). To seal their bond of friendship, the Scriptures relate, the crown prince and the former sheepherder recited vows of loyalty, and Jonathan gave David his own robe and sword. In ancient Hebrew society, a special term was used to describe the sort of mutual pact or covenant that tied Jonathan and David to one another: *hesed*, or loyal love. As author Jerry Landay explains in his book *David: Power, Lust, and Betrayal in Biblical Times*:

> Hesed was a unique personal covenant made binding in the presence of the Lord. In other oriental societies such private pacts had been sealed ritually in blood. In Israel the parties to a compact of loyal love exchanged garments or weapons, which symbolized the admired qualities of each friend. In this way David and Jonathan made their covenant of friendship—an unbreakable pledge . . . that transcended

[rose above] self-serving considerations of ego, ambition or power.

Saul had always been especially fond of Jonathan and was in the habit of sharing all of his important concerns and plans with the crown prince. Yet, despite his close relationship with his heir, the king seems to have been unaware of the depth of Jonathan's friendship with David. Consequently, as his jealousy and hostility toward David grew following David's marriage to Michal, Saul made a shocking confession to Jonathan. He wanted his son-in-law dead, and since David seemed to be all but invincible on the battlefield, Saul intended to have him assassinated. Horrified, Jonathan immediately searched out David and warned him to stay away from the royal court until he had had a chance to talk more with his father. Jonathan then returned to Saul and begged him to spare his friend's life: "The king should not sin against his servant David, because he has not sinned against you, and because his deeds have been of good service to you," Jonathan argued, "for he took his life in his hand when he attacked the Philistine, and the Lord brought about a great victory for all Israel. You saw it, and rejoiced; why then will you sin against an innocent person by killing David without cause?" (1 Samuel 19:4–5). Saul, deeply moved by his eldest son's concern for his friend, promised that David would not be harmed and moreover, he could remain at court for as long as he chose.

A CLOSE CALL FOR DAVID

Saul's reconciliation with his son-in-law proved short-lived, however. As David's popularity and fame among the Israelites continued to grow in the wake of his latest military crusade against the hated Philistines, Saul's envy and distrust of the younger man reached new heights. Forgetting his pledge to his son entirely, Saul resolved to rid himself of David once and for all. Under the cover of night, the king sent several guards to

David and Michal's home with orders to ambush and kill his son-in-law as soon as David came out of the house the following morning. Luckily for David, Michal somehow managed to get wind of her father's murderous plan. After helping David to slip out of a back window, she placed a large household idol in her husband's bed. Arranging a handful of goat's hair at the head, she carefully covered the life-size statue with a cloth. The next morning, when David failed to emerge, the king's guards became suspicious and cornered Michal. Michal told them that her husband was sick in bed and must not be disturbed under any circumstances. Michal's deception quickly came to light after the guards pushed their way into David's bedchamber and discovered the idol. Confronted with her deceit by Saul, Michal lied once again, claiming that David had threatened to kill her unless she helped him to escape.

As Jonathan Kirsch points out in *King David: The Real Life of the Man Who Ruled Israel*, one odd aspect of the story of David's late-night escape and Michal's deception is the fact that the couple kept an idol in their home in the first place:

> 'Thou shalt have no other gods before me' is the first of the Ten Commandments, and the second commandment is even more specific: 'Thou shalt not make unto thee a graven image, nor any manner of likeness, [and] thou shalt not bow down unto them, nor serve them, for I the Lord thy God am a jealous God.' . . . Yet the Book of Samuel preserves a casual reference to the presence of graven images in the home of an Israelite couple—and no ordinary couple at that! Somehow, the biblical author who tells the tale of how Michal aided and abetted David in his flight from King Saul found nothing worthy of comment in the fact that the household of the king's daughter was supplied with teraphim [a Hebrew term for idols] or that Michal was perfectly comfortable in using them to trick her father and conceal her husband's

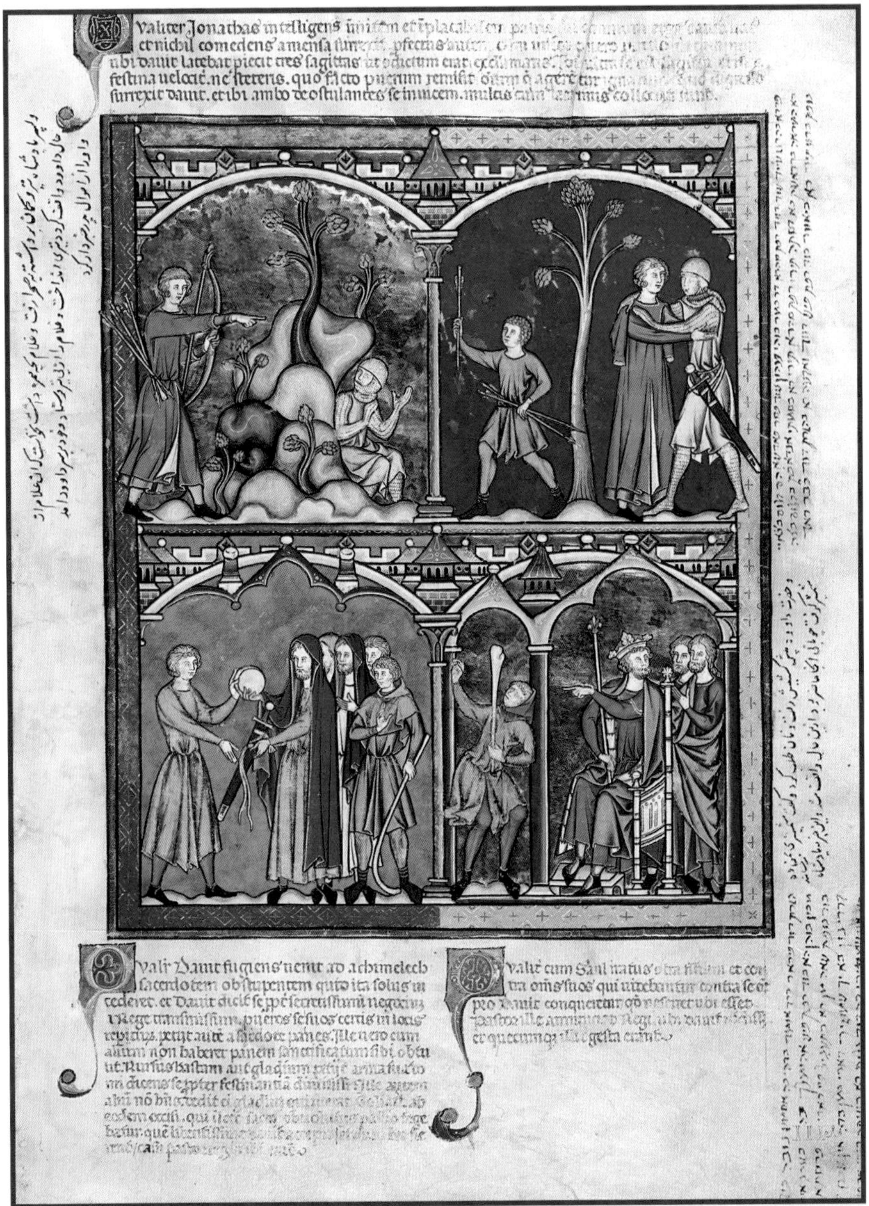

Jonathan's close relationship with David caused him to betray Saul's trust by informing his friend of the king's secret plan to have the popular warrior assassinated. When it became clear to Jonathan that Saul's opinion of David would not change, the crown prince advised David to go into hiding *(above)*.

escape. Thus, a stray line of biblical text confirms that 'God's anointed' was at liberty to indulge in religious practices that are explicitly condemned in later passages of the Bible.

"HE SHALL SURELY DIE"

After his narrow escape from the king's guards, David decided to leave Gibeah for Ramah, where he found sanctuary with the elderly Samuel. David did not stay with the high priest for long, however. Despite everything that had happened between him and the king, David dreamed of reconciling with Saul. So he sneaked back into the capital to ask for Jonathan's help in figuring out just how serious the king really was about killing him. Jonathan, who was also hopeful that his father and best friend could still heal their poisoned relationship, agreed to test the king's determination to get rid of David.

David and Jonathan decided to schedule the test for a major religious festival, the annual feast of the new moon. David had faithfully attended the three-day-long feast in Gibeah in the past, and the king made it clear that he expected his son-in-law to be there again this year. Fearful that Saul might be laying a trap for him, David had no intention of showing up for the celebration, however. Instead, he planned to hide out in the hills just outside of the royal capital. According to the plan that the two friends worked out, when Saul asked where David was, Jonathan would tell him that he had given his friend permission to travel to Bethlehem. David, he would explain, wanted to take part in a ritual sacrifice with his own family instead of attending the feast with the king at Gibeah. Then Jonathan was to report back to David regarding his father's reaction to this news. "If he says, 'Good!' it will be well with your servant [meaning David]; but if he is angry, then know that evil has been determined by him," David told Jonathan (1 Samuel 20:7).

Saul, who had in fact been secretly planning to have David killed as soon as he set foot in Gibeah, was furious when

Jonathan told him that David was in Bethlehem and the crown prince himself had approved his friend's journey there. "You son of a perverse, rebellious woman!" Saul screamed at his oldest child and heir. "Do I not know that you have chosen the son of Jesse to your own shame. . . . For as long as the son of Jesse lives upon the earth, neither you nor your kingdom shall be established. Now send and bring him to me, for he shall surely die" (1 Samuel 20:30–31). When Jonathan dared to ask exactly what David had done to deserve such malice, the king flew into a rage and hurled his spear at the prince.

Able to easily sidestep his father's hastily thrown spear, Jonathan emerged unhurt from his encounter with the king. Yet the crown prince was deeply humiliated by his parent's vicious actions and words. Early the next morning he slipped away from the palace to the hillside where David had been hiding and urged his friend to run for his life. "Go in peace," Jonathan said to David, "since both of us have sworn in the name of the Lord, saying, 'The Lord shall be between me and you, and between my descendants and your descendants, forever' " (1 Samuel 20:42). Then the friends went their separate ways. Jonathan headed forlornly back to Gibeah and his father, and David resolutely turned away from the royal capital, toward the rugged hills of what is today southern Israel. From that point on, both men abandoned all hopes of reconciliation between David and the king.

CHAPTER

5

On the Run

AFTER PARTING FROM JONATHAN IN THE HILLS OUTSIDE OF GIBEAH, DAVID decided to travel to the nearby town of Nob, where he hoped to obtain some much-needed provisions as he began his new life as a fugitive. According to the Book of Samuel, Nob was the site of a major Hebrew religious shrine during Saul and David's era.

HOLY BREAD AND THE SWORD OF GOLIATH

Once in Nob, David headed straight for the great shrine to Yahweh, where he met a priest by the name of Ahimelech. Although Ahimelech immediately recognized David as the famous military hero and son-in-law to the king, at first he refused the young man's request for provisions. The only food in the shrine was holy bread, explained Ahimelech, 12 loaves of specially prepared wheat bread set aside by the priests as a symbolic offering to Yahweh.

But David was not one to give up easily. Claiming to be on a secret mission for King Saul, he persuaded Ahimelech to turn over the blessed loaves. Next, the Bible relates, David asked the priest for a sword or spear: "Because the king's business required haste," David lied (he had not taken the time to collect his own weapons before rushing out of the royal capital). In response, Ahimelech made a startling offer: "The sword of Goliath the Philistine, whom you killed in the Valley of Elah, is here wrapped in a cloth behind the ephod [a kind of robe or gown worn by Hebrew priests]; if you will take that, take it, for there is none here except that one." David, who apparently had no idea that the sword he used to behead Goliath during their famous battle had fallen into the possession of the priests at Nob, answered the priest curtly. "Give it me," David ordered Ahimelech, and a moment later he and the sword had disappeared (1 Samuel 21:8–9).

MASS MURDER

Unfortunately for Ahimelech and his fellow priests, one of Saul's attendants, a native of the neighboring kingdom of Edom named Doeg, happened to be in Nob during David's brief visit there. Doeg observed with interest the fugitive exiting the shrine carrying several loaves of bread and a sword. When the Edomite informed the king of what he had seen, Saul exploded in rage. More than 80 priests served at the Nob shrine, and Saul ordered every one of them to travel to the royal court at Gibeah at once.

Calling Ahimelech before him, the king demanded, "Why have you conspired against me, you and the son of Jesse, by giving him bread and a sword, and by inquiring of God for him, so that he has risen against me, to lie in wait, as he is doing today?" (1 Samuel 22:13). Although Ahimelech tried to defend himself, pointing out that he had no reason to doubt the word of the king's own son-in-law, Saul was unmoved by his words. He accused the priest of deliberately aiding and abetting an enemy of the kingdom and ordered his immediate execution on grounds of treason. Then the king turned to his guards and commanded them to execute all of Nob's other holy men as well: "Turn and kill the priests of the Lord, because their hand also is with David," he decreed, "they knew that he fled, and did not disclose it to me" (1 Samuel 22:17).

Saul's guards, however, could not bring themselves to harm the priests of Yahweh. At that moment, Doeg the Edomite came to the king's rescue and volunteered his services as an executioner. Perhaps because he had not been born into the Hebrew faith, Doeg seemed to have no qualms about spilling a Hebrew priest's blood. According to the Scriptures, by the end of the day the Edomite had personally slaughtered Ahimelech and 84 of his fellow holy men. Yet Saul's thirst for revenge had still not been satisfied. He commanded his servant Doeg to go to the town of Nob and slay every man, woman, and child he encountered, as well as all of the villagers' cattle and sheep.

A DESPERATE PLAN

In the meantime David, figuring he stood little chance of eluding the posse Saul had surely sent after him, formulated a desperate plan. He would journey westward to the Philistine city of Gath and beg its ruler, King Achish, for refuge from their mutual enemy, the king of Israel. Yet David had somehow failed to take into consideration just how famous he still was in Gath, which was, after all, the hometown of his celebrated Philistine opponent Goliath. When David was presented to King Achish, his wary counselors reminded the monarch of David's run-ins with the Philistine army at the Valley of Elah and on numerous other battlefields over the past several years. "Isn't he the one about whom the Israelites used to sing, 'Saul has killed his thousands, and David his ten thousands'?" they asked suspiciously (1 Samuel: 21:13).

Suddenly fearful for his life, David pretended to be mentally ill: "He scratched marks on the doors of the gate, and let his spittle run down his beard," the Scriptures report (1 Samuel 21:14). As David had hoped, King Achish and his advisers were rattled by his strange behavior. The Philistines, like most ancient pagan peoples, blamed mental disease on the anger of vengeful gods. Psychological illness, they believed, was the gods' way of punishing someone for an especially evil deed or thought. Therefore, the safest course of action to follow with a mentally disturbed individual was to keep as far away from him or her as possible. Any attempt to interfere with the object of heaven's wrath, it was reasoned, would only serve to anger the gods further with potentially disastrous results for the entire community.

"Look," Achish scolded his guards as David continued to drool and talk nonsense, "you see the man is mad; why then have you brought him to me? Do I lack madmen, that you have brought this fellow to play the madman in my presence? Shall this fellow come into my house?" (1 Samuel 21:14). To David's enormous relief, the chastened guards hustled him out of Achish's palace, never stopping until he was on the far side of the city gates.

DAVID AT THE CAVE OF ADULLAM

Having given up on the idea of seeking sanctuary with the Philistines—at least for the time being—David fled from Gath to a large cave in the hills of southwestern Israel known in the Bible as the Cave of Adullam. Somehow word of David's location reached his relations in Bethlehem, about a day's journey northeast of Adullam. Resolved to aid their son and sibling in any way they could, David's parents and brothers journeyed to his underground hideout. Soon after their arrival, dozens of other supporters began flocking to the cave. "Everyone who was in distress, and everyone who was in debt, and everyone who was discontented gathered to him; and he became captain over them. Those who were with him numbered about four hundred," the First Book of Samuel reports (1 Samuel 22:2).

Among David's growing band of followers was a priest named Abiathar. The son of Ahimelech, David's murdered helper from Nob, Abiathar had managed to slip away from Saul's palace before Doeg could run him through with his sword. When David heard what Saul had done to Ahimelech and the other holy men of Nob, he had immediately offered Abiathar asylum. "Stay with me, and do not be afraid," David told the young priest, "for the one who seeks my life seeks your life; you will be safe with me" (1 Samuel 22:23).

Yet, despite his assurances to Abiathar, David worried that the cave of Adullam was neither a safe nor a healthful home for his aged parents. David therefore traveled eastward across the Jordan River to neighboring Moab to ask King Mizpeh if he would allow Jesse and his wife (whose name is never mentioned in the Bible) to reside in his kingdom. In Moab, David figured, they would be well out of the vengeful Saul's reach. It might seem surprising, particularly after his experiences with the Philistine king Achish, that David would approach one of Israel's traditional enemies for assistance. According to the Scriptures, however, David had an important tie to Moab: his great-grandmother Ruth had been born there. To David's relief, King Mizpeh, no doubt swayed by David's Moabite ancestry, generously agreed to his request.

LIBERATING KEILAH

Shortly after David returned from Moab to the Cave of Adullam, a follower by the name of Gad advised the fugitive leader to move to an even more remote corner of Israel in the kingdom's southern reaches. The place that Gad had in mind was deep within the hilly, barren region of Israel known as Judah, after the tribe to which David and his family belonged. According

Hiding from Saul and the Philistines, David discovered the Cave of Adullam in the southwestern mountains of Israel. When his family heard of his whereabouts, they gathered at the cave with a large group of David's supporters *(above)*.

to the Book of Samuel, Gad was a prophet of Yahweh. Consequently, David took Gad's opinion very seriously, and with the prophet's blessing, led his by now 600-strong army of supporters to the forest of Hereth in the Judahite wilderness.

Not far from David's new hideout in the forest of Hereth lay the Israelite town of Keilah. Located on the western border of Judah, Keilah was a favorite target of Philistine raiding parties. Recently, the Philistine marauders had become ever more brazen in their attacks on the settlement, even pilfering the townspeople's harvested grain right off the floor of their threshing facilities. David asked Yahweh if he and his band should attempt to rescue Keilah from its attackers. According to the

Scriptures, God answered David's question with a resounding "yes" and promised that he and his men would triumph over the Philistine enemy. Although David immediately relayed this encouraging message to his followers, the men were extremely reluctant to undertake such a risky mission. "Look, we are afraid here in Judah," they said, "how much more then if we go to Keilah against the armies of the Philistines?" (1 Samuel 23:3). So David asked for the Lord's guidance one more time, the Bible relates, and once again Yahweh—presumably speaking through the priest Abiathar or the prophet Gad—promised his protection. Following the second message from Yahweh, David's soldiers finally caved in to their leader's wishes.

After a hard and bloody fight, David's army crushed the Philistine forces and saved the inhabitants of Keilah. Many Philistines were slaughtered in the battle, the Bible reports, and David and his band came into possession of some useful plunder in the form of the enemy's cattle. But when Saul learned that David had liberated Keilah, instead of being grateful for his help in Israel's ongoing war against the Philistines, he saw an excellent opportunity to finally eliminate the man he hated above all others. Since Keilah was a walled city, the king reasoned, it would be easy for his troops to surround and trap David and his soldiers there. "God has given him into my hand," Saul gloated, "for he has shut himself in by entering a town that has gates and bars" (1 Samuel 23:7).

JONATHAN PAYS DAVID A VISIT

Before Saul's forces could reach Keilah, however, David somehow got wind of Saul's plan. Uncertain of whether to stay and fight or flee, he turned to Abiathar for guidance. Was the royal army really on its way, he wanted to know, and could he trust the people of Keilah to back him if the king's forces laid siege to the town? Saul's army was indeed marching toward Keilah, Abiathar said. As for the townspeople, he prophesized, they would surely betray David to save their own skins. Taking the priest's warning seriously, David rushed his army out of Keilah, journeying to what the Scriptures call the "Wilderness of Ziph." Archaeologists believe David's new hideout was some 10 miles southeast of Keilah, in the craggy backcountry of southern Judah.

While David was in the Wilderness of Ziph, the crown prince decided to slip down to Judah and pay his old friend a surprise visit. Saul was as determined as ever to eliminate him, Jonathan confided to David. The king even planned to personally lead an expedition to hunt him down. Yet Jonathan had come to Ziph to encourage as well as to warn his friend: "Do

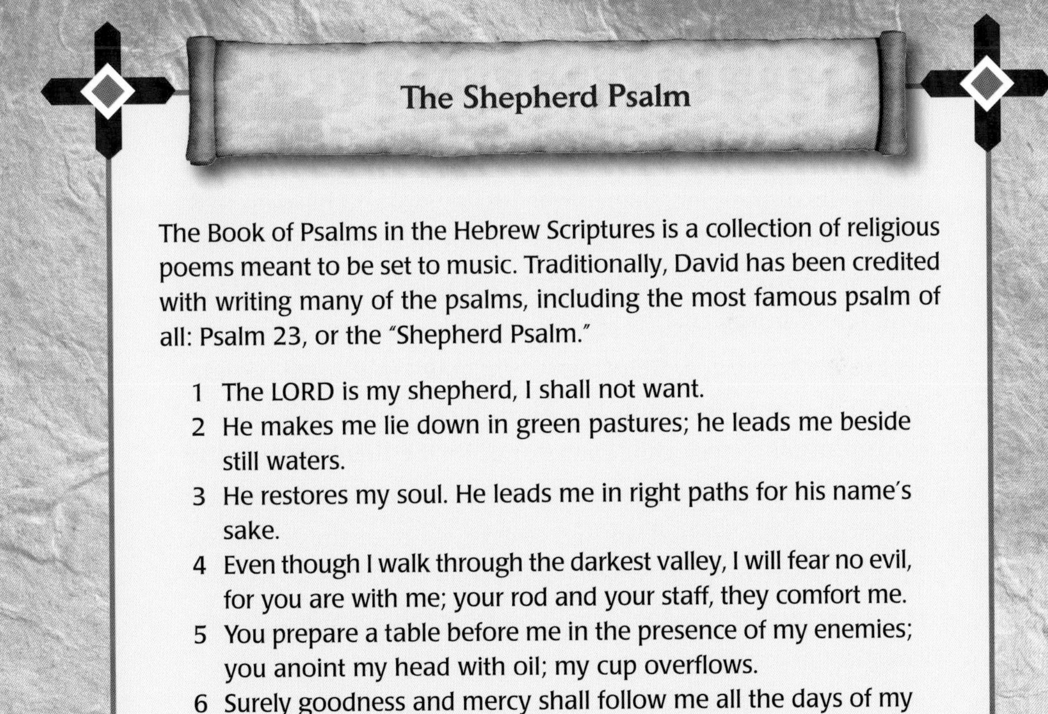

The Shepherd Psalm

The Book of Psalms in the Hebrew Scriptures is a collection of religious poems meant to be set to music. Traditionally, David has been credited with writing many of the psalms, including the most famous psalm of all: Psalm 23, or the "Shepherd Psalm."

1 The LORD is my shepherd, I shall not want.
2 He makes me lie down in green pastures; he leads me beside still waters.
3 He restores my soul. He leads me in right paths for his name's sake.
4 Even though I walk through the darkest valley, I will fear no evil, for you are with me; your rod and your staff, they comfort me.
5 You prepare a table before me in the presence of my enemies; you anoint my head with oil; my cup overflows.
6 Surely goodness and mercy shall follow me all the days of my life, and I shall dwell in the house of the LORD my whole life long.

not be afraid," he told David, "for the hand of my father shall not find you." Then, the Scriptures relate, the heir to the throne made a startling prediction: "You shall be king over Israel," he told David, "and I shall be second to you" (1 Samuel 23:17).

A NARROW ESCAPE

Shortly after Jonathan's secret journey south, Saul himself arrived in Judah with a large army. He headed straight for David's newest encampment, high on a hill above the village of Maon, about three miles south of the Wilderness of Ziph. According to the Bible, Saul found out about David's most recent hideaway from several of the fugitive's former neighbors in Ziph. Whether the Ziphites betrayed David in hopes of receiving a reward or simply out of loyalty to the crown is unknown.

Saul's troops quietly approached the bluff where David was hiding from the side opposite the Bethlehemite's camp. Dividing his army into two units, the king then sent them around both sides of the cone-shaped hill. Just as Saul and his men were about to close the circle and trap David in his hillside refuge, however, a royal messenger suddenly appeared. There had been a major Philistine raid, he reported breathlessly, and Saul's army was urgently needed. Reluctantly, the king abandoned his pursuit of David to focus on the Philistines. In the wake of this uncomfortably close call, David and his men fled eastward to a ruggedly beautiful place on the fringes of the Judahite desert called En-gedi. Nestled on the western shore of the Dead Sea, En-gedi is surrounded by steep cliffs honeycombed with caves. It was in these caves that David and his followers made their new headquarters.

DAVID SPARES SAUL'S LIFE

Yet once again David's new hideout did not remain a secret for long. After routing the Philistine raiders, Saul learned from his

In these illustrations, David is seen saving the inhabitants of Keilah from the Philistines. Although this was an enormous blow against the longtime enemy of his kingdom, King Saul was less than grateful for David's military triumph at Keilah.

informants that his son-in-law had fled to En-gedi. Assembling a force of 3,000 elite warriors, Saul marched up into the cliffs to find his foe. At one point in the search Saul ducked into a cave in order to relieve himself. By remarkable coincidence, the king had chosen the very cave where David was hiding. "David and his men," the Scriptures relate, "were sitting in the innermost parts of the cave" when Saul entered (1 Samuel 24:3). When they caught sight of the king, David's followers begged him to slay Saul while he had the chance. But David angrily refused, declaring that since Saul had been anointed king by Yahweh's command, no person had the right to take his life. Only God could determine when the right time had come for Israel to have a new ruler.

David could not resist pulling a prank on the unsuspecting king, however. While the king was relieving himself, David sneaked up behind him and cut off a corner of the royal cloak with his sword. When Saul began heading for the mouth of the cave a few moments later, David suddenly called out to him: "My lord the king!" Then, boldly approaching the startled monarch, David bowed deeply and demanded:

> Why do you listen to the words of those who say, 'David seeks to do you harm'? This very day your eyes have seen how the Lord gave you into my hand in the cave; and some urged me to kill you, but I spared you. I said, 'I will not raise my hand against my lord; for he is the Lord's anointed.' See, my father, see the corner of your cloak in my hand; for by the fact that I cut off the corner of your cloak, and did not kill you, you may know for certain that there is no wrong or reason in my hands. I have not sinned against you, though you are hunting me to take my life. May the Lord judge between me and you! May the Lord avenge me on you; but my hand shall not be against you . . . (1 Samuel 24:8–12)

Hearing David's words, Saul was overcome by feelings of shame and remorse. "You are more righteous than I; for you have repaid me good, whereas I have repaid you evil," he confessed tearfully. "Now I know that you will surely be king. . . . Swear to me therefore by the Lord that you will not cut off my descendants after me, and that you will not wipe out my name from my father's house," Saul pled. "So David swore this to Saul," the Scriptures relate, and he and his army went home to Gibeah (1 Samuel 24:17–22). David, still wary of the man whose obsessive jealousy had nearly cost him his life so many times, did not follow Saul back to the royal court but instead remained in the Judahite wilderness.

CHAPTER

6

Surviving

DAY-TO-DAY SURVIVAL WAS A CONSTANT CHALLENGE FOR DAVID AND HIS followers in southern Israel's rugged backcountry. In their ongoing quest to secure food for themselves and their families, the fugitives were often forced to rely on the generosity of their neighbors in Judah. When the locals were reluctant to help out, David was not above using strong-arm tactics to obtain the provisions he needed, as the well-known biblical story of David, the rich farmer Nabal, and his independent-minded wife, Abigail, illustrates.

DAVID AND NABAL

According to the Book of Samuel, David first became aware of the wealthy Nabal from his troops. They had stumbled upon the farmer's huge flocks of sheep and goats near the town of Carmel in southern Judah. Nabal, David soon learned, was the richest man for miles around, the owner of vast farm fields and livestock numbering into the thousands. Figuring that Nabal could easily afford to share some of this enormous bounty with his own hungry followers, David ordered 10 of his soldiers to pay a visit to Nabal and ask him for a donation.

David was very specific regarding what he wanted his envoys to say to Nabal, the Bible relates: "Thus you shall salute him: 'Peace be to you, and peace be to your house, and peace be to all that you have. . . . Now your shepherds have been with us, and we did them no harm, and they missed nothing, all the time they were in Carmel. Ask your young men, and they will tell you. Therefore let my young men find favor in your sight. . . . Please give whatever you have at hand to your servants and to your son David' " (1 Samuel 25:6–8). The central point of this speech, writes Robert Alter in *The David Story*, "is that David's men did not permit themselves to take any of Nabal's flock, and perhaps also that as armed men they defended Nabal's people against marauders. But there is a certain ambiguity [a situation that can be interpreted in more than one way] as to whether David was providing protection out of sheer good will or conducting a protection racket in order to get the necessary provisions for his guerilla band."

The Bible does not reveal whether Nabal believed David's men had actually provided his flocks and herders with valuable protection against thieves, or whether he figured they were trying to exhort food from him as part of what is often referred to as a "shakedown." At any rate, Nabal stubbornly refused to hand over the food. "Who is David?" the rich landowner sneered. Observing that runaway slaves had been roaming the Judahite countryside lately, Nabal pointed out that he knew nothing about the messengers' or their leader's background: "Shall I take my bread and my water and the meat that I have butchered . . . and give it to men who come from I do not know where?" he asked disdainfully.

ENTER ABIGAIL

David was incensed when his envoys returned to camp and told him what Nabal had said. Vowing to kill the haughty farmer along with every other male in his household, David ordered 400 of his troops to march with him to Nabal's estate.

In the meantime, one of Nabal's shepherds quietly approached his master's wife, Abigail, and informed her of everything that had happened. Described in the Scriptures as clever and beautiful, Abigail was also a remarkably independent-minded woman at a time when wives were expected to submit to their spouses in all matters. If her husband would not pay David and his men for protecting the family's livestock, then she would have to do it herself, Abigail resolved. Moving as quickly as she could, she gathered together "two hundred loaves, two skins of wine, five sheep ready dressed, five measures of parched grain, one hundred clusters of raisins, and two hundred cakes of figs," the Scriptures report (1 Samuel 25:18). Then, without saying a word to Nabal, she loaded the food and drink onto donkeys and set off in the direction of David's camp.

As Abigail approached the hill where David had his hideout, she saw the fugitive and his troops marching directly toward her down the road. When David discovered that Abigail was Nabal's wife, he declared bitterly: "Surely it was in vain that I protected all that this fellow has in the wilderness, so that nothing was missed of all that belonged to him; but he has returned me evil for good" (1 Samuel 25:21). By the following morning, he vowed, not a single male on Nabal's estate—young or old—would still be alive.

Horrified, Abigail begged David to abandon his vengeful plan. Her husband was an "ill-natured" and foolish fellow, she

Upon learning of Napal's refusal to help David, Abigail provided food and drink for David's soldiers. Her generosity, along with an impassioned speech urging David to give up his murderous plan for getting back at the stingy Nabal, caused David to abandon his vow to kill all the males in Nabal's house.

declared, whose words should not be taken seriously. "Now let this present that your servant has brought to my lord be given to the young men who follow my lord," she said, pointing to the large amount of food and wine she had brought with her.

"Please forgive the trespass [sin] of your servant," Abigail added humbly, "for the Lord will certainly make my lord [meaning David] a sure house, because my lord is fighting the battles of the Lord; and evil shall not be found in you so long as you live" (1 Samuel 25:28). Much impressed by Abigail's emotional speech, David agreed to take the provisions and turn back to his camp. According to the Bible, he even thanked her for saving him from his own worst inclinations: "Blessed be the Lord, the God of Israel, who sent you to meet me today!" he said. "Blessed be your good sense, and blessed be you, who have kept me today from bloodguilt and from avenging myself by my own hand!" (1 Samuel 25:32–3).

DAVID'S WIVES

Abigail waited until the following morning to tell her husband about David's chilling threat and the food and wine she had given him. When Nabal heard Abigail's disturbing story, the Scriptures relate, "his heart died within him; he became like a stone" (1 Samuel 25:37). Ten days later he was dead, possibly from a massive heart attack or stroke.

Less than two weeks after Nabal's death, David asked Abigail to marry him. Abigail, who appears to have harbored little affection for her late husband, promptly accepted the fugitive's proposal. Accompanied by five maids, the wealthy widow followed David back to his hillside camp where a wedding ceremony was performed. Soon after, the First Book of Samuel relates, David took another bride—a woman named Ahinoam from the nearby town of Jezreel. As for his wife Michal, the Scriptures note, when David went into hiding, Saul had his daughter's first marriage dissolved and then married her off to another man by the name of Paltiel.

The fact that David was married to two women at once might seem shocking, but polygyny—having multiple wives—was an accepted custom among the Hebrews. The term "polygyny," rather than the more familiar word "polygamy"—meaning having multiple spouses—is the most accurate one for describing the marital practices of the Israelites. In ancient Israel a woman could not legally have more than one husband at a time, whereas a man was allowed to have as many wives as he could support. Although the taking of multiple wives was permitted in ancient Israel, historians believe that most Israelite men were monogamists (meaning they had just one spouse at a time). Polygyny seems to have been practiced chiefly by kings and a few biblical patriarchs such as Abraham and Israel.

DAVID SPARES SAUL'S LIFE A SECOND TIME

After David spared Saul's life in the cave at En-gedi, the repentant king had slunk back to Gibeah, apparently having given up his vendetta against the younger man for good. But once he was back home, Saul's obsessive jealously and distrust of David soon returned. Accompanied by a large army, the king again marched south to Judah to hunt down and kill his rival.

Late one night, having been alerted to Saul's whereabouts by his scouts, David sneaked over to the king's encampment to spy on his tormentor. Accompanying David on his reconnaissance mission was his loyal nephew Abishai. Saul and his troops, exhausted after a long day's march, were sleeping heavily. Abishai saw an excellent opportunity to dispose of his uncle's arch-enemy once and for all. Let me pin the king to the ground with his own spear, he begged David. Yet once again David refused to have any part in the murder of the Lord's anointed king. Instead, he crept up next to the sleeping monarch and quietly removed his spear and water jar. Then he and Abishai stationed themselves high on a ridge overlooking Saul's camp and waited for daybreak.

As the royal troops began to stir the next morning, David boldly called out from his hillside hiding place to Saul's cousin and chief bodyguard, Abner: "Are you not a man? Why then have you not kept watch over your lord the king?" he taunted the startled warrior. "See now, where is the king's spear, or the water jar that was at his head?" (1 Samuel 26:15–16).

Struggling to awaken, Saul thought he recognized his former son-in-law's voice in the distance. "Is that your voice, my son David?" he called out. "It is . . . , my lord, O king," David replied, adding: "Here is your spear, O king! Let one of the young men come over and get it! The Lord rewards everyone for his righteousness and his faithfulness; for the Lord gave you into my hand today, but I would not raise my hand against the Lord's anointed." Perhaps fearing that David's forces had surrounded the camp and were waiting for a word from their commander to launch an attack, Saul tried to make amends with his old enemy. "I have done wrong; come back, my son David, for I will never harm you again," he vowed, "because my life was precious in your sight today; I have been a fool, and have made a great mistake" (1 Samuel 26:17; 21–23). Yet David had no more faith in the sincerity of Saul's repentance now than he had had during their meeting in the cave at En-gedi. For the moment, he would return to his hideaway in the Judahite wilderness. But in the wake of this last close call with Saul, David had concluded that he must leave the kingdom of Israel altogether. Soon David, his wives, and his 600 troops and their families were headed to Gath, the headquarters of Achish, one of the five kings who ruled Philistia.

SEEKING REFUGE WITH THE PHILISTINES

Much had changed since the last time David had sought help from the Philistine ruler. On his first visit to Gath shortly after going on the run, David had been alone and frightened. After the king's advisers recognized him as Goliath's killer, in order to save his life he had pretended to be crazy. In the years since his first meeting with Achish, however, David had not only raised a large army but had become even more famous throughout

Philistia as King Saul's chief enemy than as Goliath's slayer. On the theory that "my enemy's enemy is my friend," King Achish decided to give David another chance.

When David asked Achish to let him and his band take over one of his kingdom's outlying towns, the king generously offered David the border village of Ziklag. Archaeologists can only guess at Ziklag's location, but some scholars believe the town lay several miles north of the modern city of Beersheba in the Negev (or Negeb) Desert. According to the Bible, after relocating to Ziklag, David supported himself and his followers by pillage and plunder, attacking unsuspecting settlements and carrying off their sheep, cattle, donkeys, and other livestock. King Achish wanted David to run raids on nearby Israelite outposts, using Ziklag as his bases of operations. David, however, had no intention of harming his own people. While Achish thought he was plundering Judahite towns, David was actually carrying out his raids much farther south and east, in remote settlements inhabited by Israel's traditional rivals such as the nomadic Geshurite and Gizrite tribes, the Bible relates. David planned his raids with coldhearted precision to ensure that not a single man or woman was left alive to inform the Philistine king of what he was really up to.

After David had lived in Ziklag for about a year, the Philistines decided to launch a major invasion of their hated rival, Israel. King Achish, who had been completely fooled by David's lies, invited the fugitive and his men to join his own forces in routing the Israelites. Apparently figuring that he and his troops would simply change sides during the heat of battle, David agreed to assist Achish and marched to the main Philistine camp at Aphek, a three-day journey north of Ziklag. Shortly after David and his men arrived at Aphek, Achish and the four other Philistine kings held a war counsel. Deeply distrustful of the former Israelite war hero, Achish's fellow kings ordered the Gath ruler to send David and his troops home to Ziklag at once. "He shall not go down with us to battle," they vowed, "or else he may became an adversary to us in the battle. . . . Is this not David, of whom they sing to one another in dances, 'Saul has killed his thousands, and David his ten thousands'?" (1 Samuel 29:4–5).

Saul and the Medium

As the Philistines began amassing their troops on Israel's western border in preparation for their planned invasion, Saul became increasingly anxious. This time around, he worried, his army might not be able to turn back the kingdom's aggressive neighbors. He repeatedly sought guidance from God on how to conduct the war. Yet Yahweh was silent, the Bible reports. In desperation, Saul turned to a medium for help, a non-Hebrew woman from the city of Endor. Mediums were thought to have the ability to communicate with the spirits of the deceased.

Saul had become obsessed with the idea of seeking military advice from the prophet Samuel, who had died recently. Turning to a medium for assistance was awkward for Saul, however, since in keeping with the Law of Moses, he had outlawed the practice of necromancy (communicating with the dead) throughout his kingdom. Therefore, when Saul went to see the medium from Endor, he disguised himself so that she would not know that she was speaking with the king.

When Saul asked the woman to conjure up Samuel's spirit, the medium said she could see the old prophet rising up out of the ground. Samuel, she said, was furious about being disturbed. Nonetheless, Saul commanded the medium to ask Samuel what ought to be done about the newest Philistine threat. To Saul's horror, rather than offering him military advice, Samuel's ghost angrily predicted the king's death and the death of his sons in battle: "The Lord will give Israel along with you into the hands of the Philistines," the prophet declared, "and tomorrow you and your sons shall be with me; the Lord will also give the army of Israel into the hands of the Philistines." Upon hearing this terrible message, the Scriptures report, "Saul fell full length on the ground, filled with fear" (1 Samuel 28:19–20).

DISASTER AT ZIKLAG

When David journeyed to the Philistine camp to join King Achish, he took every one of his 600 troops with him. As it turned out, this was a terrible mistake. Three days after the Philistine leadership ordered them home, David and his soldiers finally arrived in Ziklag, exhausted by their long trek and eager to reunite with their families. To the men's horror they discovered only smoldering, empty ruins where their homes had once stood. Clearly, a raiding party from one of the nomadic tribes that roamed the Negev Desert had attacked the town and carried off all its residents. David's distraught soldiers were so embittered by what they considered to be their commander's inexcusably poor judgment in leaving the town undefended that they threatened to execute him by stoning.

Through his priest Abiathar, David asked Yahweh if he and his men would be able to track down the raiders and recover their wives and children. When God answered in the affirmative, David convinced his disgruntled army to set out into the Negev in pursuit of their missing loved ones. Before long the band spotted a young Egyptian lying face down on the sand and barely breathing. After they gave the man water and food, he revived sufficiently to tell them that he had been a slave of the raiders who attacked Ziklag. He had watched them raze the town, steal the livestock, and kidnap the women and children. When he had fallen ill on the way back to the thieves' camp, the Egyptian related, his heartless master had simply abandoned him in the desert to perish from thirst and hunger. If David promised to spare his life, he would lead the rescue party to the nomads, the slave declared.

A short time later, David, his men, and their Egyptian guide quietly approached the marauders' camp. The nomads were drinking and feasting merrily, celebrating the success of their latest raid. David cautiously decided to wait until dusk to launch an attack. After a long and grueling fight, the Israelites finally managed to slaughter all of the raiders, except a handful who

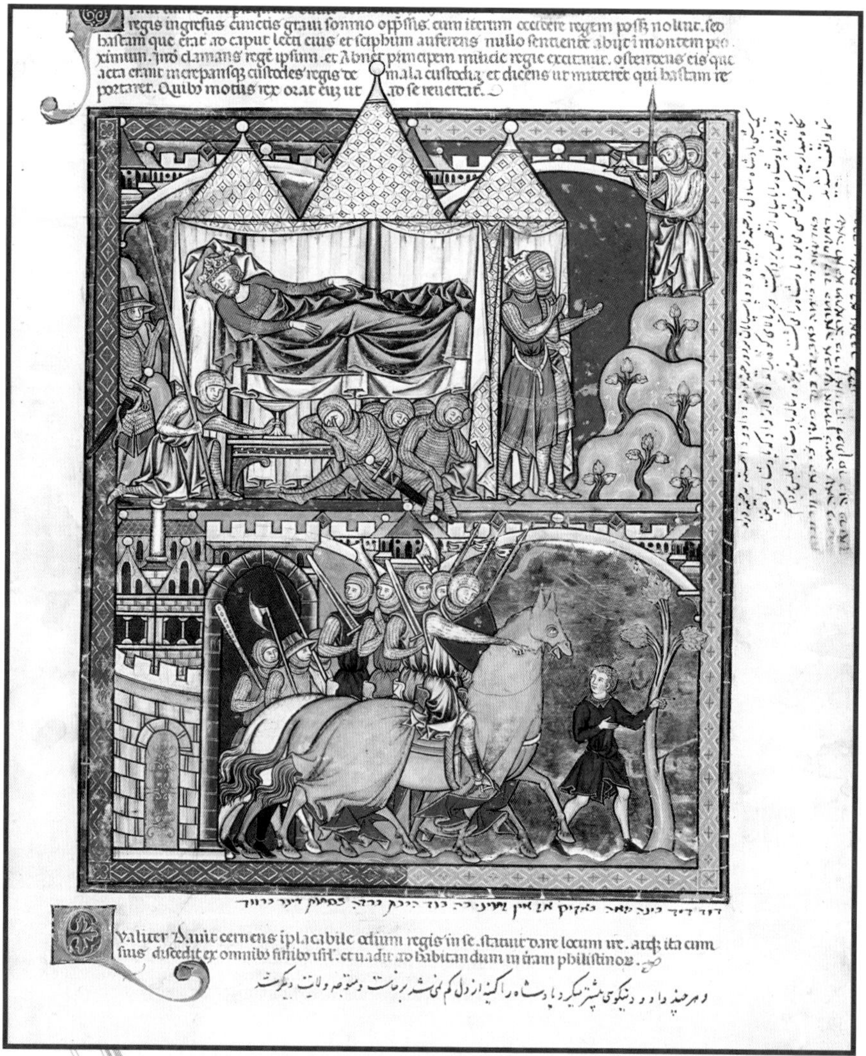

Despite sparing Saul's life a second time, David soon found himself being hunted by the monarch again. Though he knew Saul wanted him dead, David refused to kill the king; instead, as Saul and his forces were sleeping at their encampment in Judah, David took Saul's personal spear and water jug *(above)*.

escaped into the desert on camels. To the men's relief every one of the kidnapped wives and children was found alive and unharmed. The victorious Israelites also gained much valuable plunder from the dead raiders in the form of sheep, cattle, and other livestock.

After dividing a portion of the plunder equally among his troops, David sent out the remainder of the booty to anyone who had assisted him while he was in the Judahite wilderness. Significantly, he also sent cattle and sheep to the elders of each of Judah's major towns and cities. With each of the gifts he included a note: "Here is a present for you from the spoil of the enemies of the Lord" (1 Samuel 30:26). The Book of Samuel does not comment regarding David's motives in sharing his valuable plunder with Judah's local leadership. But if his intention was to win the Judahites' goodwill and support, David would not be disappointed in the months and years ahead.

CHAPTER

7

King of Israel

WHILE DAVID AND HIS MEN WERE RESCUING THEIR FAMILIES IN THE Negev Desert, many miles to the north in Israel's Jezreel Valley, King Saul and his army were preparing to repel the Philistine invaders. The three oldest of Saul's four sons—Abinadab, Malkishua, and the crown prince, Jonathan—accompanied their father into battle.

THE DEATHS OF SAUL AND JONATHAN

The contest between the Israelites and the larger and better-equipped Philistine army at Jezreel Valley was over almost before it began. In growing desperation, Saul watched his soldiers panic and run before their powerful enemy. With victory in sight, the Philistines focused their attention on the Israelite king and his three sons, eventually closing in on their prey on the slopes of Mount Gilboa on the valley's eastern fringes. Jonathan was the first to die, followed by his younger brothers Abinadab and Malkishua. Then a Philistine arrow struck Saul. Resolved that his foes should not take him alive, the wounded king commanded his armor-bearer to slay him. "Draw your sword and thrust me through with it," he ordered. Terrified of Yahwah's wrath, the armor-bearer refused to kill the Lord's anointed king. Moments later, the Book of Samuel reports, "Saul took his own sword and fell upon it" (1 Samuel 31:4).

According to the Bible, Saul was driven to suicide by a terrible fear. If he allowed himself to be taken alive, the Philistines would take a cruel delight in humiliating and tormenting the king of Israel before they finally executed him. The Philistines' degrading treatment of Saul's corpse and the bodies of his three slain sons indicates that the king's fears were well grounded. The day after their victory, the Philistines collected the four royal corpses from the battlefield, chopped off their heads, and triumphantly pinned their bloody torsos to the wall of Beth Shan, a city just to the west of the Jezreel Valley.

When reports of the desecration of Saul's body reached the Israelite settlement of Jabesh-Gilead nine miles away from Beth Shan, the villagers rallied in support of their deceased monarch. Years earlier, King Saul had saved Jabesh-Gilead from the brutal King Nahash of Ammon. Now the town was determined to give its defender a proper burial. Under cover of darkness, a courageous band of villagers crept up to the Beth Shan wall and removed the mangled corpses of the royal family. Back in Jabesh-Gilead, the slain men's remains were cremated and buried under a tamerisk [a type of cedar] tree and the people mourned and fasted for the king and his sons for seven days.

DAVID AND THE AMALEKITE

Within days of Saul's death a stranger arrived in Ziklag looking for David. When he was brought before the fugitive leader, the man fell face down on the ground in front of him, a traditional Middle Eastern way of showing respect to a monarch. Although he was an Amalekite by birth, the stranger told David, he had fought with the Israelite army against the Philistines in the Valley of Jezreel.

"How did things go? Tell me!" David asked urgently. The Israelites fled before the larger Philistine force, the man replied, and Saul and Jonathan had both been killed. According to the account in the Second Book of Samuel, the Amalekite then went on to relate a much different version of the wounded Saul's final moments than the one described in the First Book of Samuel: "I happened to be on Mount Gilboa," the man said,

> and there was Saul leaning on his spear, while the chariots and horsemen drew close to him. When he looked behind him, he saw me and called to me. I answered, 'Here sir.' And he said to me, 'Who are you?' I answered him, 'I am an Amalekite.' He said to me, 'Come, stand over me and kill me; for convulsions have seized me, and yet my life still lingers.' So I stood over him and killed him, for I knew that he could not live after he had fallen. I took the crown that was on his head and the armlet that was on his arm, and I have brought them here to my lord. (2 Samuel 1:5–10)

The discrepancy between the accounts of Saul's death on Mount Gilboa in the two books of Samuel is never explained in the Bible. However, many biblical scholars think that the Amalekite was lying. He invented the story about killing Saul in order to gain favor with David, whom he assumed would be Israel's next monarch now that Saul and his three eldest sons were dead. Convinced that David would praise him for his role in Saul's death, the Amalekite was stunned when David instead ordered his immediate execution. "Your blood be on your head," David told the terrified man, "for your own mouth has testified against you, saying, 'I have killed the Lord's anointed' " (2 Samuel 1:16).

At Jezreel Valley in northern Israel, a large Philistine army routed the forces of King Saul, who was accompanied by three of his four sons, including Jonathan. Jonathan and his two brothers were quickly killed in the fighting. Afraid of what the Philistines would do if they found him alive, Saul threw himself on his sword to avoid potential humiliation and torture.

KING DAVID

On the day that they first heard the news of the king and crown prince's deaths, the Bible says, David and his men "mourned and wept, and fasted until evening for Saul and for his son Jonathan . . . because they had fallen by the sword" (2 Samuel 1:12). Moved to eloquence by the passing of the Lord's anointed ruler and his best friend, David composed an elegy (a song or poem that mourns and praises the dead) in Saul and Jonathan's honor. Despite Saul's persecution of him, David remembered only the king's best qualities in his elegy, praising his military

David's Elegy for Saul and Jonathan (2 Samuel 1:19–27)

Your glory, O Israel, lies slain upon your high places!
  How the mighty have fallen!

Tell it not in Gath,
  proclaim it not in the streets of Ashkelon;
  or the daughters of the Philistines will rejoice,
  the daughters of the uncircumcised will exult.

You mountains of Gilboa,
  let there be no dew or rain upon you,
  nor bounteous fields!
  For there the shield of the mighty was defiled,
  the shield of Saul, anointed with oil no more.

From the blood of the slain,
  from the fat of the mighty,
  the bow of Jonathan did not turn back,
  nor the sword of Saul return empty.

skill, courage, and strength. "Greatly beloved were you to me," David wrote emotionally of his loyal defender, Jonathan, "your love to me was wonderful, passing the love of women" (2 Samuel 1:26).

With Saul dead, David immediately began to think of returning home to Israel. According to the Scriptures, when David asked Yahweh where he should settle, God told him to go to the city of Hebron. Located approximately 20 miles south of Bethlehem, Hebron was the traditional capital of David's tribal homeland of Judah. Because it was widely believed to be

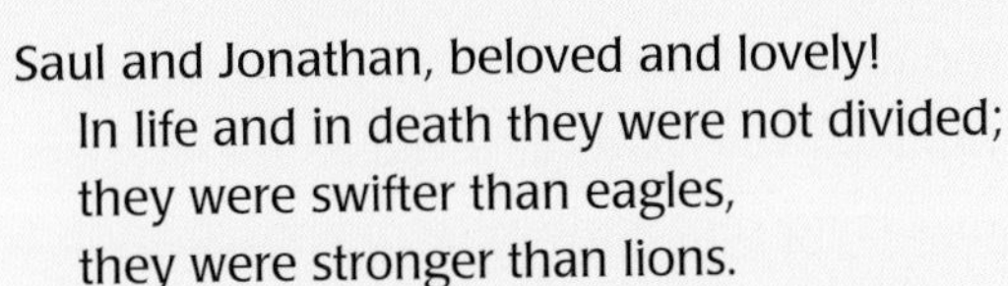

Saul and Jonathan, beloved and lovely!
In life and in death they were not divided;
they were swifter than eagles,
they were stronger than lions.

O daughters of Israel, weep over Saul,
who clothed you with crimson, in luxury,
who put ornaments of gold on your apparel.

How the mighty have fallen
in the midst of the battle!
Jonathan lies slain upon your high places.

I am distressed for you, my brother Jonathan;
greatly beloved were you to me;
your love to me was wonderful,
passing the love of women.

How the mighty have fallen,
and the weapons of war perished!

the burial place of several Bible patriarchs, including Abraham, Hebron was also one of ancient Israel's holiest sites.

Accompanied by his 600 soldiers and their families, David left his adopted town of Ziklag and set out for Hebron. Soon after his arrival in the sacred city, a delegation of elders from across southern Israel came to Hebron to crown their region's favorite son as king of Judah. In choosing the Bethlehemite as their leader, the elders were probably influenced by David's proven military skills. They may also have been swayed by David's generosity in sharing with them the booty he had confiscated from Ziklag's nomad attackers. As it turned out, however, David was not the only man to be proclaimed king of the Israelites after Saul's death.

A KINGDOM DIVIDED

Shortly after his coronation ceremony, David heard about the brave men of Jabesh-Gilead who had retrieved Saul's mutilated body from Beth Shan. David sent a message of appreciation to the northern Israelite town, saying "May you be blessed by the Lord, because you showed this loyalty to Saul your lord, and buried him! Now may the Lord show steadfast love and faithfulness to you!" David also informed the people of Jabesh-Gilead of his lofty new status within Judah: "And I too will reward you because you have done this thing. Therefore let your hands be strong, and be valiant; for Saul your lord is dead, and the house of Judah has anointed me king over them" (2 Samuel 2:5–7).

The people of Judah may have recognized David as their king, but in the northern half of Israel where Jabesh-Gilead was located, his right to succeed Saul was being challenged by the late monarch's own relatives. Shortly after Saul's death, Abner, Saul's cousin and the commander of the royal army, had declared the deceased king's youngest son, Ishbaal (or Ishbosheth), king of all Israel's tribes, including the Judahites. For the next seven and a half years, the Hebrew kingdom would be split into two warring sections. In the south, Judah remained steadfastly loyal to David. In the north—popularly referred to as Israel, even though it did not include the lower portion of the old Israelite kingdom—Ishbaal and his right-hand man, Abner, ruled.

ABNER, ISHBAAL, AND DAVID

According to the Scriptures, during the more than seven-year-long civil war that wracked the Promised Land following Saul's death, most of the fighting consisted of hand-to-hand contests between small groups of elite warriors from David's and Ishbaal's armies. Under Ishbaal's inept leadership, the Bible notes, militarily and politically the north grew "weaker and weaker." In contrast, under David's able direction, the south became "stronger and stronger" (2 Samuel 3:1). Finally, Ishbaal's top general, Abner, lost all patience with the incompetent man he had helped make king. For the sake of his country's future, Abner decided, he must desert Ishbaal and back David as ruler of a reunited Israel. Abner fired off a secret message to the Bethlehemite, offering to help him secure the support of the northern tribes. "Make your covenant with me," he wrote, "and I will be bring all Israel over to you" (2 Samuel: 3:12–13).

Abner's offer was certainly tempting. Yet until he could see just how much influence the general actually had within Israel, David shrewdly refused to commit himself to anything. After giving it some thought, David decided to make a bargain with Abner: He would accept the general's proposal only if Abner could retrieve David's first wife, Michal. Michal was living somewhere in Israel with her husband, Paltiel, the spouse whom Saul had selected for Michal years earlier when David first fled the royal court. The Bible does not reveal David's motives for trying to renew his relationship with Michal. However, some scholars have suggested that David wanted Saul's daughter in his harem in order to strengthen his claim to the Hebrew kingship. It seems unlikely that love had anything to do with David's campaign to get Michal back, since by this point in his life he was married to no less than six different women: Abigail, Ahinoam, Maacah, Haggith, Abital, and Eglah.

When Abner quickly restored Michal to David—despite the protests of her devoted husband Paltiel, the Bible reports—the impressed king agreed to work with his rival's turncoat general. Abner then sent word to the elders of the northern tribes promising that together he and the great warrior-king David would safeguard Israel from the Philistines and their other enemies. The tribal leaders, who obviously trusted and respected Abner far more than they did Ishbaal, wasted no time in transferring their support to David.

DAVID BECOMES KING OF ISRAEL

Abner's influence with the northern elders made him a tremendous asset to David in his ongoing struggle for the leadership of a united Israel. Nonetheless, David's commander in chief, Joab, was incensed when he learned that Abner and David were now allies. Early in the civil war, Abner had killed Joab's brother Asahel in battle, stabbing him with such violence that his spear penetrated the young man's chest and came out his back. Joab had long dreamed of taking revenge on his brother's killer. Hence, the next time that Abner came to Hebron to see David, Joab cornered the general at the city gate and stabbed him to death. David, well aware of Abner's high standing in the north, was horrified. He issued a public statement strongly denying his own involvement in the killing and insisted that Joab publicly mourn his victim.

The murder of his chief adviser threw Ishbaal into a complete panic. Dismayed by the king's weakness, two of Ishbaal's officers plotted to assassinate him and clear the way for David to rule all of Israel without delay. Sneaking into the royal bedchamber, the assassins murdered the peacefully sleeping king in his own bed. Taking along Ishbaal's severed head as gruesome proof of their bloody deed, the men then journeyed to the royal court at Hebron. "Here is the head of Ishbaal, son of Saul, your enemy, who sought your life," they told David, "the Lord has avenged my lord the king this day on Saul and on his offspring" (2 Samuel 4:8). But instead of rewarding the boastful soldiers as they had clearly expected him to do, David denounced them as murderers:

> As the Lord lives, who has redeemed my life out of every adversity, when the one who told me, "See, Saul is dead," thought he was bringing me good news, I seized him and killed him at Ziklag—this was the reward I gave him for his news. How much more then, when wicked men have killed a righteous [innocent] man on his bed in his own house! And now shall I not require his blood at your hand, and destroy you from the earth?

With that David ordered his guards to slay the flabbergasted assassins. After executing the men, the Scriptures report, the guards "cut off their hands and feet, and hung their bodies beside the pool at Hebron" (2 Samuel 4:9–12). In sharp contrast to his treatment of the two regicides (king killers), David ordered that Ishbaal's remains be given an honorable burial in the same tomb that housed the body of his former general, Abner. David's swift execution of Ishbaal's assassins and his respectful treatment of the late king's remains sent an unmistakable message to the northern elders: David had had nothing to do with his rival's death, even though he clearly stood to benefit from it.

CAPTURING JERUSALEM

Soon after Ishbaal's burial, the heads of the northern tribes traveled to Hebron to anoint David as their new king. For the first time in more than seven years, Israel was once again under the rule of a single sovereign. Now, David believed, the reunited kingdom needed a new capital. What he had in mind was a capital whose location would reassure his northern subjects that he meant to treat the north and south equally, despite his own roots in the southern region of Judah. Because of its location on the border between the northern and southern tribal territories of Israel, David decided that the city of Jerusalem on Mount Zion was the perfect site for Israel's royal capital.

There was one problem with David's choice of Jerusalem as his new seat of power, however. Although located in the very heart of Israelite territory, Jerusalem had long been under the control of a Canaanite people called the Jebusites. Wresting Jerusalem from the Jebusites would be difficult, David realized, because natural defenses as well as man-made fortifications surrounded the city on every side. As Jerry Landay notes in his biography of David, Jerusalem "was all but impregnable. . . . It lay on a narrow spur of rock that sprang from the main ridge line of central Canaan. The spur was bounded by precipitous [steep] ravines on the west, south and east. Many an army exposed on the slopes below had been torn to pieces by withering fire from the great towers that rose over the walls, or dashed itself hopelessly against the great honey-pale walls of the local Jerusalem stone anchored deeply in solid rock."

Determined to claim the city on Mount Zion as his own, David came up with an ingenious plan for getting around Jerusalem's defenses. According to the account of Jerusalem's capture in the Second Book of Samuel, David ordered an advance party of commandos to sneak into an underground tunnel that carried fresh water from the nearby Spring of Gihon through the city walls and straight into the heart of Jerusalem. Taken off guard by David's cunning, the Jebusites were easily routed by the Israelite forces. The change of regime in Jerusalem seems to have gone smoothly, perhaps because David did not expel the conquered city's residents or destroy their homes and other personal property. Shortly after capturing Jerusalem, David had a stone and cedar palace built where he could direct the affairs of state and reside with his numerous wives and children. In accordance with a long-standing tradition among Middle Eastern monarchs, he also renamed Israel's new capital for himself, dubbing it "the City of David."

THE ARK OF THE COVENANT

David wanted his new capital city to be more than just Israel's administrative center. He also wanted it to be the kingdom's religious center. To that end he made Jerusalem the headquarters of the kingdom's two high priests: Abiathar, who had joined David's band of fugitives many years earlier after Saul massacred his fellow priests of Nob, and Zadok, a high priest under Saul who threw his support to David following Saul's death.

A second way in which David strengthened Jerusalem's role as the spiritual, as well as the political, heart of Israel was to transfer to Jerusalem the most sacred relic of his faith, the Ark of the Covenant. In Hebrew the word *ark* means "box" or "chest." The Ark of the Covenant was a rectangular box fashioned from acadia wood and roughly measuring 3 3/4 feet long by 2 feet wide and 3 inches deep. It held the two stone tablets inscribed with the Ten Commandments that the Israelites believed Yahweh had given Moses in the Sinai Desert. Since the Israelites were originally a nomadic people, the ark was fitted with rings and staves on either side that permitted it to be carried from place to place.

Moving the Ark of the Covenant from its current resting place in the Judahite town of Kiriath-Jearim, about eight miles away from Jerusalem, to his new capital turned out to be a much longer process than David had expected. While the ark was being transported on an ox-drawn cart over a bumpy road, it began to totter. One of the attendants assigned to take the relic to Jerusalem grabbed onto the wobbling box to keep the ark from falling. Touching the holy box anywhere except on the rings and staves by which it was carried about was strictly forbidden. Moments after the attendant placed his hand on the ark, the

After securing Jerusalem for his kingdom, David moved the Ark of the Covenant to his new capital city *(above)*. The arrival of the most sacred relic of the Jewish faith was marked by processions of music and joyous celebration.

Bible relates, the man suddenly fell to the ground, dead. David was so unnerved by this incident that he decided to put off the remainder of the journey to Jerusalem for three months.

Finally the ark reached the gates of Jerusalem, accompanied by the proud king and a huge procession of musicians. As the parade wound its way through the streets of the capital, David danced with joyful abandon before the ark. David's exuberant dancing earned him the disdain of his wife Michal, who thought such behavior unbecoming to a king. David, however, was unapologetic. As long as his dancing pleased God, he said, it did not matter in the least if his wife or anyone else disapproved of it.

After placing the Ark of the Covenant in a tent like the one that had sheltered it in Kiriath-Jearim, David asked the prophet Nathan to speak to Yahweh regarding a subject that was very close to his heart. He wanted to know if God would let him build a grand temple in Jerusalem to house the ark. Nathan, however, told David that God did not approve of him overseeing the building of so holy a structure. As a result of the many battles he had fought in, the king's hands were too bloodstained for such a sacred task, Nathan said. The job of constructing a great temple to Yahweh in Jerusalem, Nathan prophesized, would fall to David's son and successor. Nonetheless, the Lord was very pleased with David's faithfulness, Nathan assured his master. Indeed, he was so pleased that he had made an extraordinary pledge to David. The Lord would preserve the king's "house" or dynasty until the end of time: "Your house and your kingdom shall be made sure forever before me," Yahweh promised, "your throne shall be established forever" (2 Samuel 7:16).

CHAPTER

8

Great Victories and Terrible Crimes

THE PHILISTINES WATCHED DAVID'S REUNIFICATION OF ISRAEL WITH GROW-ing concern. As a consequence of Saul's defeat at the Jezreel Valley, Philistia had taken control of a great deal of Israelite territory on the kingdom's western fringes. With a strong political and military leader now in charge of Israel for the first time in nearly eight years, the Philistines feared that the land they had gained in their final battle against King Saul would be lost.

DEFEATING THE PHILISTINES AND BUILDING AN EMPIRE

Determined to eliminate Israel's powerful new king, the Philistines launched two major military campaigns against Israel, the first one shortly after David was crowned. Both campaigns took place just to the west and southwest of Jerusalem. According to the Bible, David and the large, highly trained Israelite army he assembled struck back hard against the kingdom's invaders. By the end of the second campaign, David had successfully pushed the Philistine armies back to their traditional coastal territories, ending Philistia's threat to his kingdom for good.

After defeating the Philistines, David next turned his attention eastward, according to the Bible. David expanded Israelite territory and made his kingdom into a significant power in the Middle East through a series of successful military campaigns against his neighbors across the Jordan River. The Scriptures report that during the early years of his reign, David's army subjugated the Ammonites, Moabites, and Edomites in the east, and in the northeast took over part of the kingdom of Aram near present-day Damascus, Syria. In order to secure Israel's northern border, the king also relied on diplomacy, signing a peace treaty with Hiram, the king of Tyre, an important Phoenician trading center on the coast of what is today Lebanon.

DAVID AND BATHSHEBA

One spring when most of his army was away on a campaign, David noticed an attractive woman in the public baths near his palace. David was so impressed by the woman's beauty that he sent a servant to the bathhouse to find out her name. Her name was Bathsheba, daughter of Eliam and wife of Uriah the Hittite, one of David's warriors, the servant reported. The Hittites were an ancient people who lived in what is today the nation of Turkey. Bathsheba's husband, however, was probably not a foreigner but rather an Israelite of Hittite ancestry, notes Robert Alter, because Uriah was a good Hebrew name meaning "the Lord is my light."

By the time he first laid eyes on Bathsheba, David had as many as two dozen concubines (mistresses) and spouses. But this did

With Jerusalem in his possession and the throne unchallenged, David was declared king during a coronation ceremony *(above)*. After the ceremony, he quickly planned and executed two military campaigns to purge his kingdom of invaders, a move that also eliminated further conflicts with the Philistines.

not stop him from pursuing the wife of his soldier. The king summoned Bathsheba to his palace, the Bible relates, and had sexual relations with her. Soon after this encounter, Bathsheba discovered she was pregnant. David had to be the father, she informed the king, because Uriah had been away at war for months.

David was appalled by Bathsheba's news. Adultery was a grave sin in ancient Israel. According to Hebrew tradition, it was acceptable for a man to have multiple wives and concubines. Yet having sexual relations with another man's wife was strictly forbidden. Eager to avoid a scandal, David invented an excuse to call Uriah back from the field. He figured that Uriah was bound to sleep with his wife while he was home on leave. Then the betrayed husband—and everyone else—would assume that Uriah was father of Bathsheba's baby. To David's dismay, however, Uriah insisted on spending the night at the palace in the guards' quarters. He explained that he could not go home to his comfortable bed when his fellow soldiers in the field were forced to sleep on the hard ground. David even tried plying Uriah with wine, but drunk or sober, the dutiful warrior held fast to his principles and refused to go home to Bathsheba.

DAVID REPENTS

At this point the king devised a desperate plan: He would get rid of Uriah and marry Bathsheba before the baby was due. David immediately ordered Uriah back to the field with a sealed scroll to present to Joab, his commander in chief. Unbeknownst to Uriah, the scroll commanded Joab to arrange the warrior's death. "Put Uriah in the face of the fiercest battling and draw back," David wrote, "so that he will be struck down and die" (2 Samuel 11:15). A short time later Joab sent David a message informing him that Uriah had fallen in battle. When Bathsheba heard the news, she mourned for her late husband for a suitable period of time, "and when the mourning was over,

David sent and gathered her into his house and she became his wife," the Scriptures relate (2 Samuel 11:27). Now that he and the pregnant Bathsheba were legally married, David assumed that the whole sordid ordeal was behind him.

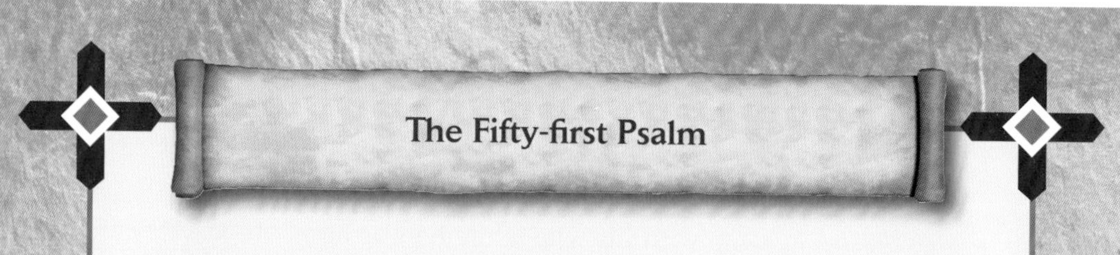

The Fifty-first Psalm

Psalm 51 is traditionally believed to have been written by David after the prophet Nathan chastised him for his adulterous affair with Bathsheba, the wife of Uriah the Hittite.

1 Have mercy on me, O God,
according to your steadfast love;
according to your abundant mercy
blot out my transgressions.
2 Wash me thoroughly from my iniquity,
and cleanse me from my sin!
3 For I know my transgressions,
and my sin is ever before me.
4 Against you, you only, have I sinned
and done what is evil in your sight,
so that you may be justified in your words
and blameless in your judgment.
5 Behold, I was brought forth in iniquity,
and in sin did my mother conceive me.
6 Behold, you delight in truth in the inward being,
and you teach me wisdom in the secret heart.
7 Purge me with hyssop, and I shall be clean;
wash me, and I shall be whiter than snow.
8 Let me hear joy and gladness;
let the bones that you have broken rejoice.

The prophet Nathan was not about to let David off the hook so easily, however. Somehow he had gotten wind of David's treachery and was thoroughly disgusted. David was an adulterer and for all intents and purposes, a murderer, Nathan bluntly

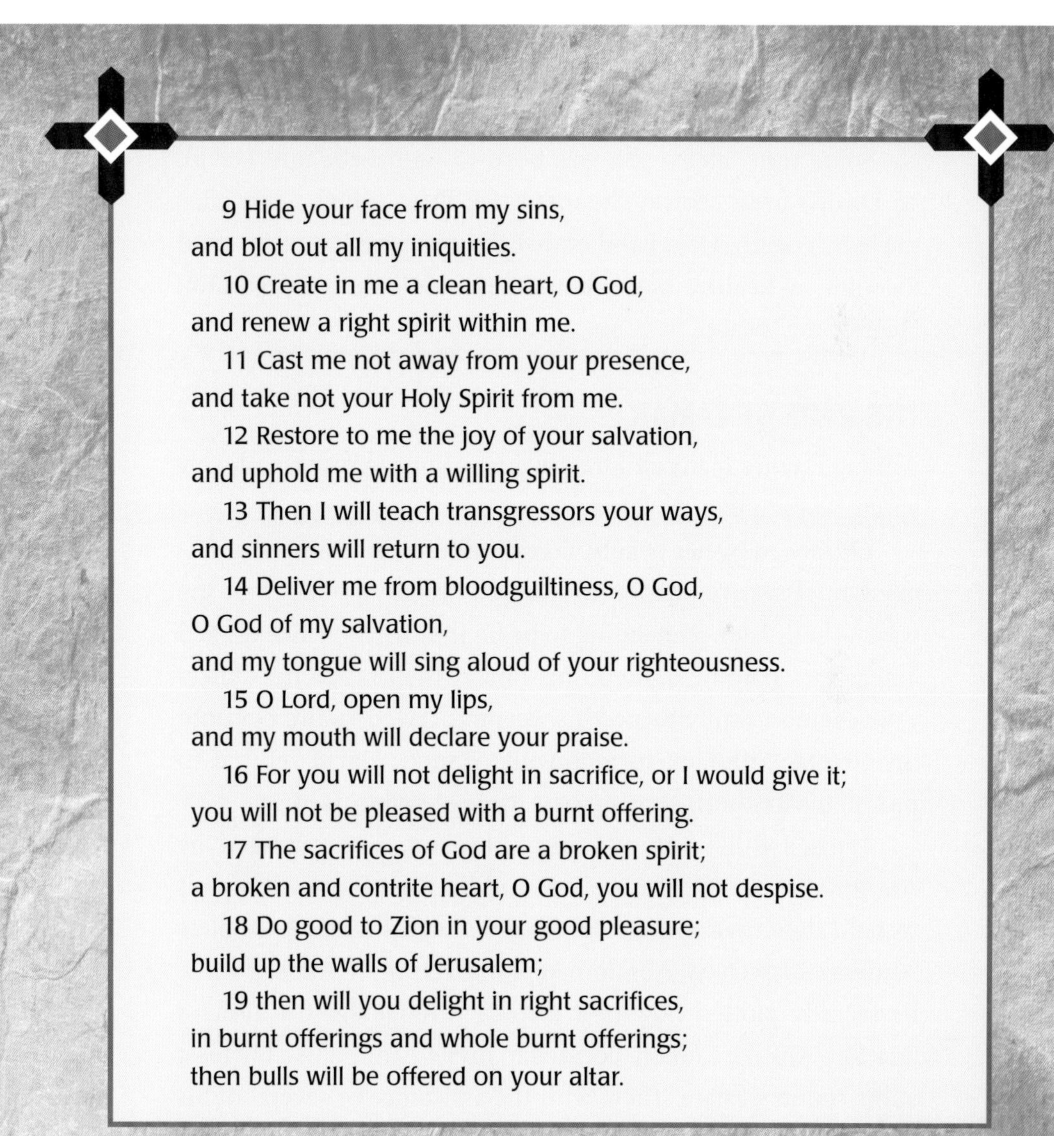

9 Hide your face from my sins,
and blot out all my iniquities.
10 Create in me a clean heart, O God,
and renew a right spirit within me.
11 Cast me not away from your presence,
and take not your Holy Spirit from me.
12 Restore to me the joy of your salvation,
and uphold me with a willing spirit.
13 Then I will teach transgressors your ways,
and sinners will return to you.
14 Deliver me from bloodguiltiness, O God,
O God of my salvation,
and my tongue will sing aloud of your righteousness.
15 O Lord, open my lips,
and my mouth will declare your praise.
16 For you will not delight in sacrifice, or I would give it;
you will not be pleased with a burnt offering.
17 The sacrifices of God are a broken spirit;
a broken and contrite heart, O God, you will not despise.
18 Do good to Zion in your good pleasure;
build up the walls of Jerusalem;
19 then will you delight in right sacrifices,
in burnt offerings and whole burnt offerings;
then bulls will be offered on your altar.

told the king. Yahweh, the prophet warned, would surely punish him for his crimes. Instead of trying to deny his wrongdoing or make excuses for himself, David took full responsibility for his mistakes and humbly admitted to Nathan and God that he had sinned. This greatly impressed Nathan, who assured the king that Yahweh had forgiven him. "Now the Lord has put away your sin; you shall not die," Nathan told David (2 Samuel 12:13). Nonetheless, Nathan declared, because of David's wicked actions his family would be plagued by many tragedies and difficulties.

Some time later a son was born to Bathsheba and David. To David's great sorrow the infant fell ill and died. Soon after the baby's death, David and Bathsheba conceived another child together: a healthy boy whom they would name Solomon, Hebrew for "peace."

THE RAPE OF TAMAR

Among David's many children by his various wives was a lovely young woman named Tamar.

Entranced by her beauty, David's eldest son, Amnon, developed an obsessive passion for Tamar, despite the fact that she was his half sister. Pretending to be ill, the crown prince tricked Tamar into coming alone to his house, then raped her. Afterward Amnon coldly turned his weeping, dazed victim out onto the streets. Although furious with Amnon, David refused to punish his firstborn son and heir for his terrible deed.

Tamar's full brother, Prince Absalom, was outraged by Amnon's treatment of his sister and by David's unwillingness to hold the crown prince responsible for his actions. To allay Amnon's suspicions, Absalom kept his feelings to himself while he secretly plotted how best to take revenge against Tamar's attacker. Absalom finally decided to invite Amnon to a big feast at his country estate. Then, with the assistance of several of his servants, Absalom murdered his sister's rapist in full view of all his guests.

Knowing that the penalty for murder was death, Absalom fled Israel and lived in exile in a faraway city for three years. David, who had now lost two sons, was brokenhearted. He brooded constantly about his estranged child, the Bible relates, and neglected his kingly duties. At last David's army commander and right-hand man, Joab, convinced the distraught king to pardon Absalom. Once Absalom returned to Israel, David's depression quickly lifted. Nonetheless, it took the king two years to completely forgive Amnon's killer and welcome him back into the royal palace.

ABSALOM'S REBELLION

What David did not realize was that Absalom had never forgiven him for failing to take Tamar's part against Amnon. Determined to destroy the king, once he returned to Jerusalem, Absalom immediately began to plot David's overthrow. Within four years of his homecoming, the handsome and charismatic prince had managed to attract an army of followers from all over the kingdom. Deciding the time was ripe to launch his rebellion, Absalom slipped out of Jerusalem and journeyed to David's former capital at Hebron. There the prince's supporters anointed him as Israel's new ruler.

When David heard that Absalom, accompanied by a sizable army, was on his way from Hebron to Jerusalem to claim the throne, the king and his court fled eastward toward the Jordan River. Since the main Israelite army was away in the field at the time, David was fearful that he and the handful of soldiers left in Jerusalem would be outnumbered and trapped in the walled city.

At the last minute, David decided to leave behind one of his oldest and wisest advisers in the capital, a man named Hushai, as a spy. When the rebel prince arrived with his army in Jerusalem, Hushai won his trust by pretending to back him against David. Hushai then counseled Absalom not to rush out of the capital in pursuit of his father. Luckily for David, Absalom heeded the older man's advice, thereby providing the king with precious time in which to raise an army. Eventually, Absalom and David's troops met in the forest of Ephraim, just east of the Jordan River. The king's soldiers fought ferociously against the rebels, slaughtering thousands of them. Ever the loving father, David commanded Joab and his other officers to "deal gently" with Absalom, however (2 Samuel 18:5).

"O MY SON ABSALOM"

Deep within the forest of Ephraim, Joab and his men spotted Absalom riding before his troops on a mule, the traditional mount for members of the Israelite royalty. As he passed under an oak tree, Absalom's long thick hair was caught fast in a low-hanging branch and he became trapped. When Joab saw Absalom dangling from the tree, he knew what he had to do. As long as the charismatic prince lived, Joab realized, he would pose a threat to David's throne. Disobeying David's order to "deal gently" with the prince, Joab drove three javelins into Absalom's chest. Then the commander and his men tossed the rebel commander's body into a large hole and piled rocks on top of it—a traditional Middle Eastern way of burying a hated enemy. When Absalom's soldiers heard that their leader was dead, the Scriptures report, they fled the battlefield at once and headed for their homes.

David was devastated when he found out what had occurred in the forest of Ephraim. It did not seem to matter to the king that his forces had successfully quelled the rebellion. All David could think about was that he had lost another child. "O my son Absalom, my son, my son Absalom!" the king wept in one of the most touching passages from the Hebrew Scriptures: "Would I had died instead of you. O Absalom, my son, my son!" (2 Samuel 18:33).

The triumphant soldiers returned to Jerusalem from Ephraim and discovered that instead of celebrating their victory,

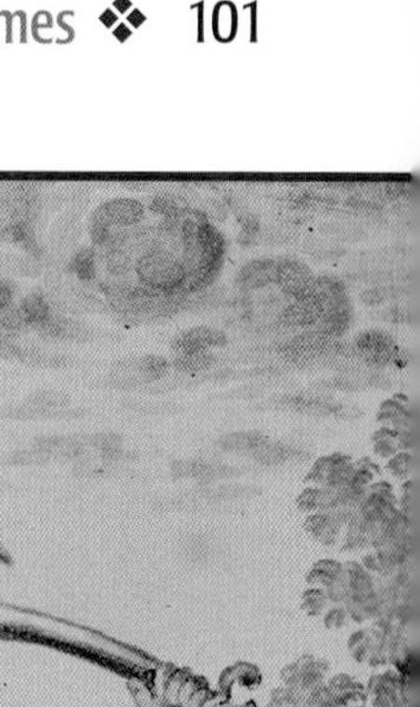

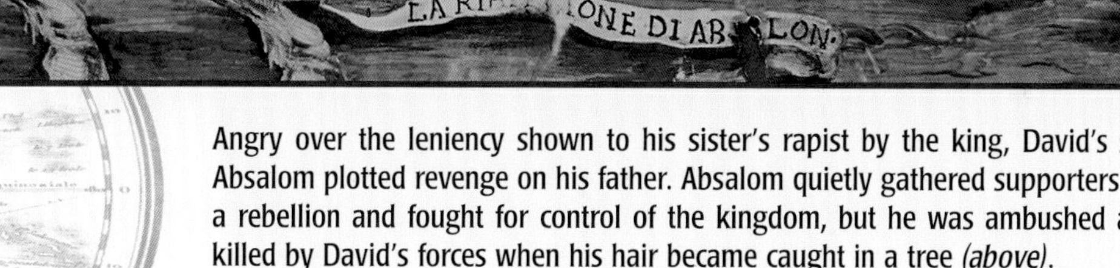

Angry over the leniency shown to his sister's rapist by the king, David's son Absalom plotted revenge on his father. Absalom quietly gathered supporters for a rebellion and fought for control of the kingdom, but he was ambushed and killed by David's forces when his hair became caught in a tree *(above)*.

the king was grieving for his dead son. Many of them became so demoralized by the king's behavior that they deserted the capital. Joab was incensed by David's seeming indifference toward his men and warned him that his entire army was likely to abandon Jerusalem if he did not get a grip on himself soon: "You have made it clear today that commanders and officers are nothing to you; for I perceive that if Absalom were alive and all of us were dead today, then you would be pleased. So go out at once and speak kindly to your servants [soldiers]; for I swear by the Lord, if you do not go, not a man will stay with you this night" (2 Samuel 19:6–7). Chastened, David went down to the city gate to congratulate the troops, much to the relief of Joab, his officers, and the residents of Jerusalem.

SHEBA'S REBELLION

In the wake of Absalom's rebellion, David was faced with the task of bringing the divided kingdom back together again. He made a particular point of traveling south to Judah to publicly forgive those in his native tribe who had backed the prince. But David's obvious concern with winning back the Judahites and his neglect of the other 11 tribes caused bitterness in the rest of Israel.

The resentment created by what many non-Judahites considered as David's favoritism toward his own tribe finally erupted into a new rebellion. After raising a small army, the insurrection's leader, Sheba ben Bichri, a Benjaminite, boldly declared himself king of all Israel except for Judah. Although David's larger forces easily quelled the revolt, Sheba managed to escape to Israel's northern fringes where he sought refuge in the border town of Abel. The people of Abel wanted nothing to do with the rebel fugitive, however. When they saw Joab and his troops preparing to besiege their town, they chopped off Sheba's head and hurled it over the wall to David's commander. With that, Joab marched back to Jerusalem to reassure his ruler that Sheba was no more and the kingdom of Israel was once again at peace.

CHAPTER

9

David's Final Years and Legacy

THE FINAL YEARS OF KING DAVID'S LIFE ARE CHRONICLED IN THE FIRST Book of Kings, which directly follows the two books of Samuel in the Hebrew Bible. When David was about 70 years old and had ruled the kingdom of Israel for just over three decades, the Book of Kings relates, his health began to fail and he became completely bedridden: "King David was old and advanced in years; and although they covered him with clothes, he could not get warm" (1 Kings 1:1). When it became obvious that the monarch's days on earth were numbered, a bitter succession struggle erupted between two influential groups, each of which backed one of David's sons, Adonijah and Solomon.

THE STRUGGLE FOR DAVID'S THRONE

As the eldest of David's living sons, Adonijah assumed that he would inherit his father's throne. Handsome, ambitious, and proud like his late half brother Absalom, Adonijah began to "exalt himself"—put on airs—as his father's physical condition worsened (1 Kings 1:5). Adonijah bragged to anyone who would listen that he would soon be king. He even began riding

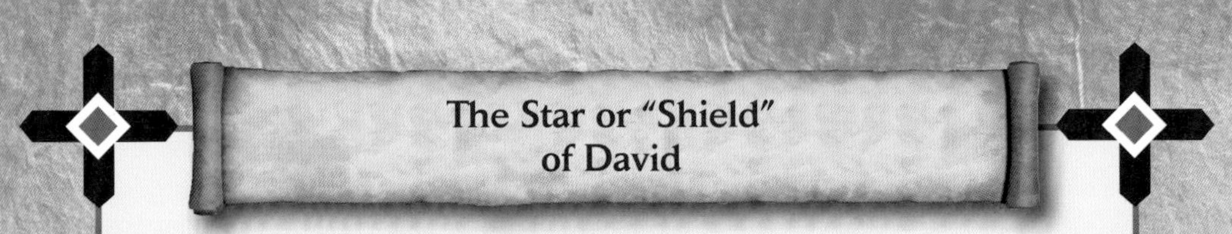

The Star or "Shield" of David

In his biography of David, *King David: The Real Life of the Man Who Ruled Israel*, Jonathan Kirsch discusses the weak connection between King David and the most famous symbol of Judaism, the six-pointed Star of David:

> . . . [T]he Star of David, the symbol that has come to signify Judaism in general and the modern state of Israel in particular, has no real connection with King David, whether we regard him as a biblical or a historical figure. Indeed, the distinctive six-pointed star first came to be associated with David among alchemists and magic-users in medieval Christian and Islamic circles, and early Jewish sources linked the star sometimes to David, sometimes to Solomon, and sometimes to neither of them. The earliest written reference to the "Shield of David" (*magen David*), as the six-pointed star is known in Jewish usage, dates only to the fourteenth century. And it was not until the nineteenth century that the Star of David came to be adopted by the Jewish community as "a striking and simple sign which would symbolize Judaism in the same way as the cross symbolizes Christianity," according to Gershom Scholem, a leading scholar of Jewish mysticism.

about Jerusalem in a chariot with 50 men running before him in attendance. Adonijah soon attracted several powerful allies, including David's army commander, Joab, and the high priest Abiathar.

Yet there were many influential people in the capital who did not want to see Adonijah ascend the throne. Led by the high priest Zadok; the captain of the palace guard, Benaiah; and the prophet Nathan, these prominent Israelites believed that Solomon, David's son with Bathsheba, would make a more effective ruler.

As time passed and the ailing king failed to publicly name his successor, Adonijah became more and more impatient. Finally he decided to take matters into his own hands. Adonijah invited his supporters and all of his brothers except Solomon to a special sacrifice to be held at a site just outside Jerusalem. Yet Adonijah had something more than just a sacrificial rite in mind. After making a burnt offering of sheep, cattle, and oxen to Yahweh, the high priest Abiathar anointed David's eldest son as the new ruler of Israel. Then Adonijah sent messengers throughout the capital to announce his coronation and invite the people to a great feast.

"THE EYES OF ALL ISRAEL ARE ON YOU"

When Nathan heard about Adonijah's anointing, he rushed back to the palace to tell Bathsheba the distressing news. Not only the throne but also her own and her son's lives could be in peril, he warned. In the ancient world a new ruler usually could be counted on to eliminate anyone he viewed as a rival to his authority. That worried Nathan because he realized that Adonijah was bound to see Solomon as his chief competitor for the crown. Go see David at once and tell him about his eldest son's treasonous behavior, the prophet advised Bathsheba. Nathan also urged Bathsheba to remind David that he had promised her that Solomon would be his successor, a claim that is not found anywhere in the Book of Samuel. Nathan's conversation with Bathsheba in the Book of Kings marks the first time that David's pledge to Bathsheba regarding the couple's son is mentioned in the Scriptures.

On leaving Nathan, Bathsheba obediently went to her husband and informed him of Adonijah's treachery. "My lord," she said,

> you swore to your servant [Bathsheba] by the Lord your God, saying: Your son Solomon shall succeed me as king, and he shall sit on my throne. But now suddenly Adonijah has become king, though you, my lord the king do not know it. He has sacrificed oxen, fatted cattle, and sheep in abundance, and has invited all the children of the king, the priest Abiathar, and Joab the commander of the army; but your servant Solomon he has not invited. But you, my lord the king—the eyes of all Israel are on you to tell them who shall sit on the throne of my lord the king after him. Otherwise it will come to pass, when my lord the king sleeps with his ancestors, that my son Solomon and I will be counted offenders. (1 Kings 1:17–21)

Nathan, who had slipped into David's bedchamber during Bathsheba's speech, backed up her story. At that very moment, he noted bitterly, Joab, Abiathar, and Adonijah were celebrating their triumph over David and Solomon. Roused to action by Nathan and Bathsheba's accusations, the king angrily vowed to his wife: "As the Lord lives, who has saved my life from every adversity, as I swore to you by the Lord, the God of Israel, 'Your son Solomon shall succeed me as king, and he shall sit on my throne in my place,' so will I do this day." With that, David called Zadok before him and commanded the high priest to anoint Solomon as king of Israel at once. "Let him enter and sit on my throne," he instructed Nathan and Zadok, "he shall be king in my place" (1 Kings 1:29–30, 35). Spurred on by his own declining health and Adonijah's determination to grab the throne out from under him, the king thus took the unusual measure of having Solomon crowned while he, David, still lived.

According to the Scriptures, David announced Solomon's hasty coronation to the people of Jerusalem with great fanfare, and the streets of the capital rang with shouts of "Long live King Solomon!" When Adonijah and his supporters realized what had happened, they scattered in fear. Adonijah, the Bible reports, rushed to the nearest altar to Yahweh and caught hold of one of its horns—the curving projections that adorned the four corners of Israelite altars. In Hebrew tradition, holding onto an altar horn was considered a plea for safety. Fortunately for Adonijah, Solomon agreed to accept his desperate bid for forgiveness. But Solomon warned his brother that if Adonijah tried to go after the Israelite crown a second time, he would surely have him killed.

DAVID'S LAST WORDS TO SOLOMON

Soon after Solomon's coronation, it became evident to David that he had very little time left. Calling his son to his bedside, the old king instructed Solomon to devote himself wholeheartedly to the service of his people and his god:

> Be strong, be courageous, and keep the charge of the Lord your God, walking in his ways and keeping his statutes, his commandments, his ordinances, and his testimonies, as it is written in the law of Moses, so that you may prosper in all that you do and wherever you turn. Then the Lord will establish his word that he spoke concerning me: "If your heirs take heed to their way, to walk before me in faithfulness with all their heart and with all their soul, there shall not fail you a successor on the throne of Israel." (1 Kings 2:2–4)

As King David's health declined, two of his sons, Adonijah and Solomon, began vying for his crown. Adonijah, the elder son, believed he had a right to the throne and arranged for a surprise coronation without including his brother. Solomon, however, received the support of the prophet Nathan and his mother, both of whom encouraged an ailing David to anoint Solomon as the rightful heir.

Then David abruptly changed the tone of his deathbed speech, giving Solomon some practical—and decidedly brutal—advice on how to handle his enemies, particularly David's own military commander, Joab. Adonijah's onetime backer, David was convinced, would always be a threat to Solomon's throne, and he needed to be disposed of as soon as possible: "do not let [Joab's] gray head go down to Sheol [the abode of the dead] in peace," he urged (1 Kings: 2:6). The dying king also wanted Solomon to eliminate a Benjaminite by the name of Shimei. Years earlier Shimei had cursed David as a scoundrel and "a man of blood" and accused him of stealing the throne from Saul's descendants (2 Samuel 16:7). Whether David was motivated by personal revenge in urging Solomon to kill Shimei or by a superstitious fear that the curse would remain in effect until its author was destroyed, is unclear.

Shortly after giving his final charge to Solomon, the Bible relates, King David breathed his last: "Then David slept with his ancestors, and was buried in the City of David," the author of the First Book of Kings wrote simply (1 Kings 2:10).

THE WEALTH AND WISDOM OF KING SOLOMON

Soon after his father's death, Solomon followed David's advice and moved to protect his crown by having both Joab and Shimei assassinated. When his brother Adonijah insolently asked if he could marry one of the king's concubines—although to claim a ruler's mistress or wife was considered the same as claiming his throne—Solomon also had Adonijah killed. With the chief potential threats to his rule eliminated, Solomon further consolidated his power by appointing his loyal supporters to the kingdom's top religious, political, and military offices.

During Solomon's long and peaceful reign, he managed to acquire extraordinary riches, most of it through trade with other Middle Eastern and North African countries. According to the First Book of Kings, King Solomon boasted "forty thousand stalls of horses for his chariots, and twelve thousand horsemen" (1 Kings 4:26). The Bible also claims that he had an astounding 700 wives and 300 concubines. Many of Solomon's marriages were to foreign princesses and appear to have been arranged to cement commercial or diplomatic treaties with other nations.

King Solomon, who is traditionally believed to be the author of the wise sayings contained in the biblical Book of Proverbs, was as famous for his sound judgment as he was for his wealth. The best-known account of his wisdom concerns two women who claimed to be the mother of the same infant boy. Solomon told the women that if they could not settle the dispute themselves, he would have no choice but to split the baby down the middle with his sword. They each could have part of the child, he said. The first woman accepted Solomon's cruel ultimatum while the second begged the king to hand the unharmed infant over to her rival instead. Realizing that a real mother would rather give up her child to another than allow him to die, Solomon gave the baby to the second woman.

THE TEMPLE OF SOLOMON AND THE HOUSE OF DAVID

Solomon reportedly oversaw the construction of many large building projects in Jerusalem and elsewhere in Israel, including a palace for himself and another for one of his wives, the daughter of the Egyptian pharaoh. His most celebrated building project, however, was the elegant temple he had erected on Mount Moriah in Jerusalem to house the Ark of the Covenant. Solomon's father had dreamt of building such a structure. But because David was a man of war, he had been told by God's spokesperson, Nathan, that his successor would have to build the temple instead. Fashioned from cedar and stone, Solomon's temple took seven years and the labor of thousands of men to complete. Solomon's Temple—also called the First Temple—was destroyed by the Babylonians of present-day Iraq in 586 B.C.,

King Solomon was able to increase prosperity throughout his kingdom while also maintaining peace. His reputation for being a wise ruler led many to his court for help in settling disputes, including one well-known argument between two women over a baby *(above)*. By threatening to split the baby down the middle with a sword, Solomon was able to draw out the truth and return the baby to its true mother.

several hundred years after the monarch's death. A Second Temple was completed on the same site in 515 B.C., and that structure survived until A.D. 70, when the Roman army razed it.

Solomon died in Jerusalem sometime during the late tenth century B.C., following a reign of nearly 40 years. His successor was his son and David's grandson, Rehoboam. Soon after Rehoboam took the throne, a rebellion broke out in the northern part of his domain, and the kingdom that David had reunited split once again into two warring halves. The northern portion, called Israel just as in King Ishbaal's day, was ruled by one of Solomon's former officers, Jeroboam, and the southern portion—Judah—was ruled from Jerusalem by Rehoboam. For the next nearly 400 years, the descendants of Rehoboam, Solomon, and David would occupy the throne of Judah. Finally in 586 B.C., 150 years after Israel fell to the warlike Assyrian Empire of northern Mesopotamia, Judah was conquered by the Babylonians, and David's dynasty along with the magnificent capital he had founded on Mount Zion, were destroyed. The city of Jerusalem would rise once more from the ashes, but the house of David would never rule Judah or Israel again.

Seemingly, the end of the royal house of David should have created a major dilemma for the faithful. After all, in the Second Book of Samuel, God, speaking through the prophet Nathan, followed up his refusal to let David build the temple in Jerusalem with an extraordinary promise to the king. David's descendants, Yahwah vowed, would rule his Chosen People forever. In the prophetic writings of the Hebrew Bible that follow the books of Samuel, Kings, and Chronicles, however, God's pledge of eternal kingship to David is given a spiritual rather than an earthly interpretation. The final ruler from the house of David, the prophets predicted, would not be a mere mortal but rather God's own son—a messiah or savior who would establish the Lord's kingdom on earth. According to followers of the Christian faith, this king-messiah is Jesus of Nazareth, whose ancestry the New Testament traces straight to David through his mother, Mary. Followers of the Jewish faith still await the arrival of the king-messiah who will come from the "stock [family] of Jesse"—David's father—in the words of the biblical prophet, Isaiah (Isaiah 11:1).

Today, some 3,000 years after his death, King David remains the focus of enormous scholarly interest and research. Because of his key role in both Christianity and Judaism as the direct ancestor of the Messiah, he also remains a spiritual icon for millions of believers around the world. Courageous and conniving, devout and lustful, humble and ambitious: warrior, poet, fugitive, and king, David is not only one of the most fascinating and complex figures in the Bible but also one of the most compelling leaders in the history of the ancient world.

CHRONOLOGY

◆◆◆

All dates are B.C. (Before Christ)

c. 1800	Hebrew people migrate to Canaan from Mesopotamia
c. 1600	Hebrew tribes depart Canaan for Egypt when famine strikes and are eventually enslaved
c. 1200	Hebrew Exodus from Egypt back to Canaan under leadership of Moses
c. 1200–1030	Israelites are ruled by the judges and by their various tribal elders
c. 1040	David, the son of Jesse, is born in Bethlehem
c. 1030	Saul becomes first king of the Israelites and the United Monarchy period begins
c. 1010–970	United Monarchy of King David
c. 970	King David dies and King Solomon's reign begins

BIBLIOGRAPHY

Alpher, Joseph, ed. *Encyclopedia of Jewish History: Events and Eras of the Jewish People*. New York: Facts On File, 1986.

Alter, Robert. *The David Story: A Translation with Commentary on 1 and 2 Samuel*. New York: Norton,1999.

Erlanger, Steven. "King David's Fabled Palace: Is This It?" *New York Times*, August 5, 2005.

Finkelstein, Israel, and Neil Asher Silberman. *David and Solomon: In Search of the Bible's Sacred Kings and the Roots of the Western Tradition*. New York: Free Press, 2006.

Halkin, Hillel. "Searching for the House of David." *Commentary*, July/August (2006): pp. 41–48.

Halpern, Baruch. *David's Secret Demons: Messiah, Murderer, Traitor, King*. Grand Rapids, Mich.: William B. Eerdmans, 2001.

The Holy Bible: New Revised Standard Version. Nashville: Thomas Nelson, 1989.

The Holy Land. Alexandria,Vt.: Time-Life, 1992.

Kirsch, Jonathan. *King David: The Real Life of the Man Who Ruled Israel*. New York: Ballantine, 2000.

Landay, Jerry M. *David: Power, Lust and Betrayal in Biblical Times*. Berkeley, Calif.: Seastone, 1998.

McKenzie, Steven L. *King David: A Biography*. New York: Oxford University Press, 2000.

Pinsky, Robert. *The Life of David*. New York: Schocken, 2005.

Porter, J. R. *The Illustrated Guide to the Bible*. New York: Oxford University Press, 1995.

WEB SITES

Jewish Heritage Online Magazine. "King David." Available online.

http://www.jhom.com/topics/david/index.html.

Kjeilen, Tore. "David," Encyclopedia of the Orient. Available online.

http://www.lexicorient.com/e.o/david.htm.

Schoenberg, Shira. "David," Jewish Virtual Library. Available online.

http://www.jewishvirtuallibrary.org/jsource/biography/David.html.

FURTHER READING

Alter, Robert. *The David Story: A Translation with Commentary on 1 and 2 Samuel*. New York: Norton,1999.

Cohen, Barbara. *David: A Biography*. New York: Clarion, 1995.

Eisler, Colin, and Jerry Pinkney. *David's Songs: His Psalms and Their Story*. New York: Dial, 1992.

Meltzer, Milton. *Ten Kings and the Worlds They Ruled*. New York: Orchard, 2002.

Segal, Lore. *The Story of King Saul and King David*. New York: Schocken, 1991.

PHOTO CREDITS

page:

3: © Bildarchiv Preussischer Kulturbesitz / Art Resource, NY
12: © Infobase Publishing
15: © Time & Life Pictures/ Getty Images
21: © Erich Lessing / Art Resource, NY
27: © Bettmann/CORBIS
33: © Art Resource, NY
39: © Erich Lessing / Art Resource, NY
45: © Cameraphoto Arte, Venice / Art Resource, NY
51: © The Pierpont Morgan Library/ Art Resource, NY
59: © National Gallery Collection; By kind permission of the Trustees of the National Gallery, London/CORBIS
63: © The Pierpont Morgan Library/ Art Resource, NY
69: © Allinari/ Art Resource, NY
76: © The Pierpont Morgan Library/ Art Resource, NY
81: © HIP / Art Resource, NY
90: © Erich Lessing / Art Resource, NY
94: © Erich Lessing / Art Resource, NY
101: © Erich Lessing / Art Resource, NY
108: © HIP / Art Resource, NY
111: © The Stapleton Collection / Art Resource, NY

INDEX

B

C

D

E

F

G

T

U

V

W

ABOUT THE AUTHORS

◆◆◆

LOUISE CHIPLEY SLAVICEK received her master's degree in history from the University of Connecticut. She is the author of more than 20 books for young people, including *Women of the American Revolution*, *Israel*, and *The Great Wall of China*. She lives in Ohio.

ARTHUR M. SCHLESINGER, JR. is remembered as the leading American historian of our time. He won the Pulitzer Prize for his books *The Age of Jackson* (1945) and *A Thousand Days* (1965), which also won the National Book Award. Schlesinger was the Albert Schweitzer Professor of the Humanities at the City University of New York and was involved in several other Chelsea House projects, including the series *Revolutionary War Leaders*, *Colonial Leaders*, and *Your Government*.